Contents

P9-BYD-468

<< THE VENETIAN
< CASINO SIGN, FREMONT CASINO

INTRODUCTION TO
LAS VEGAS

A dazzling oasis where forty million people a year escape the everyday, Las Vegas has made a fine art of indulging its visitors' every appetite. From its ever-changing architecture to cascading chocolate fountains, adrenaline-pumping zip lines and jaw-dropping stage shows, everything is built to thrill; as soon as the novelty wears off, it's blown up and replaced with something bigger and better. Not only does the city hold the largest hotels in the world, but that's pretty much all it holds; it's these extraordinary creations that everyone comes to see.

THE EIFFEL TOWER, PARIS

Best places to get a view of the Strip

Although towering hotel blocks jostle for position along the Strip, there are surprisingly few places that offer non-guests a panoramic view of the whole thing. Possibilities include the summit of the Stratosphere (but that's a little far north and not quite aligned with the Strip), and the Voodoo Rooftop Nightclub at the Rio, off to one side. So the winner is – the observation platform at the top of Paris's Eiffel Tower (see p.57), perfectly poised to look north and south along the Strip's busiest stretch, as well as west, and down, to the fountains of Bellagio.

Each hotel is a neighbourhood in its own right, measuring as much as a mile end to end; crammed full of state-of-the-art clubs, restaurants, spas and pools; and centring on what makes the whole thing possible – an action-packed casino where tourists and tycoons alike are gripped by the roll of the dice and the turn of the card.

Even if its entire urban area covers 136 square miles, most visitors see no more of Las Vegas than two short, and very different, linear stretches. Downtown, the original centre, now amounts to four brief (roofed-over) blocks of Fremont Street, while the Strip begins a couple of miles south, just beyond the city limits, and runs for four miles southwest. It's the Strip where the real action is, a visual feast where each mega-casino vies to outdo the next with some outlandish theme, be it an Egyptian pyramid (Luxor), a Roman extravaganza (Caesars Palace), a fairytale castle (Excalbur) or a European city (Paris and the Venetian).

In 1940, Las Vegas was home to just eight thousand people. It owes its extraordinary growth to its constant willingness to adapt; far from remaining kitsch and old-fashioned, it's forever reinventing itself. Entrepreneurs race to spot the latest shift in who has the money and what they want to spend it on. A few years ago the casinos realized that gamblers were happy to pay premium prices for good food; top chefs now run gourmet restaurants in venues like Bellagio and the Cosmopolitan. More recently, demand from younger visitors has prompted casinos like Wynn Las Vegas to open high-tech nightclubs to match those of Miami and LA.

The reputation Las Vegas still enjoys, of being a quasi-legal adult playground where (almost) anything goes, dates back to its early years when most of its first generation of luxury resorts were cut-throat rivals controlled by the Mob. In those days illegal profits could easily be "skimmed" off and respectable investors steered clear. Then, as now, visitors loved to imagine that they were rubbing shoulders with gangsters. Standing well back from the Strip, each casino was a labyrinth in which it was all but impossible to find an exit. During the 1980s, however, visitors started to explore on foot; mogul Steve Wynn cashed in by placing a flame-spouting volcano outside his new Mirage. As the casinos competed to lure in pedestrians, they filled in the daunting distances from the sidewalk, and between casinos.

With Las Vegas booming in the 1990s, gaming corporations bought up first individual casinos, and then each other. The Strip today is dominated by just two colossal conglomerates – MGM Resorts and Caesars Entertainment. Once you own the casino next door, there's no reason to make each a virtual prison; the Strip has therefore opened out, so that much of its central portion now consists of open-air terraces and pavilions housing bars and restaurants.

The city may have tamed its setting, but the magnificent wildernesses of the American West still lie on its doorstep. Dramatic parks like Red Rock Canyon and the Valley of Fire are just a short drive away, or you can fly to the Grand Canyon, and Utah's glorious Zion National Park makes a wonderful overnight getaway.

When to visit

Visitors flock to Las Vegas throughout the year, however the climate varies enormously. In July and August, the average daytime high exceeds 100°F (38°C), while in winter the thermometer regularly drops below freezing. Hotel swimming pools generally open between April and September only.

It's which day you visit that you should really take into account; accommodation can easily cost twice as much on Friday and Saturday as during the rest of the week.

LAS VEGAS AT A GLANCE

>> EATING

Las Vegas used to be a byword for bad food, with just the occasional mobster-dominated steakhouse or Italian restaurant to relieve the monotony of the pile-'em-high **buffets**. Those days have long gone. Every major **Strip casino** now holds half a dozen or more high-quality restaurants, many run by top chefs from all over the world. Prices have soared, to a typical minimum spend of $50 per head at big-name places, but so too have standards, and you could eat a great meal in a different restaurant every night in casinos such as **Aria**, **Bellagio**, **Caesars Palace**, the **Cosmopolitan** and the **Venetian**.

>> DRINKING

Every Las Vegas casino offers free drinks to gamblers. Sit at a slot machine or gaming table, and a cocktail waitress will find you and take your order; tips are expected. In addition, the casinos hold all kinds of bars and lounges; very few tourists venture further afield to drink. Along the Strip bars tend to be themed, as with the Irish pubs of **New York–New York** or the flamboyant lounges of **Caesars Palace**; downtown they're a bit more rough-and-ready. Note that the legal drinking age is 21 – you must carry ID to prove it.

>> NIGHTLIFE

The Strip is once more riding high as the entertainment epicentre of the world. While Elvis may have left the building, headliners like **Elton John** and **Celine Dion** attract thousands of big-spending fans night after night and all the major touring acts pass through. Meanwhile the old-style feathers-and-sequins revues have been supplanted by a never-ending stream of jaw-droppingly lavish shows by the **Cirque du Soleil**, plus the likes of the postmodern **Blue Man Group**. A new generation of visitors has been responsible for the dramatic growth in the city's clubbing scene. Casinos like the **Cosmopolitan**, the **Palms** and **Wynn Las Vegas** now boast some of the world's most spectacular – and expensive – nightclubs and ultra-lounges.

>> SHOPPING

Shopping now ranks among the principal reasons that people visit Las Vegas. **Downtown** is all but devoid of shops, however, and while the workaday city holds its fair share of suburban malls, tourists do almost all of their shopping on **the Strip** itself. Their prime destination is the amazing **Forum** at Caesars Palace, followed by the **Grand Canal Shoppes** at the Venetian and **Miracle Mile** at Planet Hollywood. There are also a couple of stand-alone malls – **Fashion Show** opposite Wynn Las Vegas, which is the most useful for everyday purchases, and the very high-end **Crystals** in CityCenter.

OUR RECOMMENDATIONS FOR WHERE TO EAT, DRINK AND SHOP ARE LISTED AT THE END OF EACH CHAPTER.

Day One in Las Vegas

1 **Jean Philippe Patisserie, Bellagio** > p.51. Head to the back of Bellagio to enjoy a morning pick-me-up and pastries while admiring the world's largest chocolate fountain.

2 **The Conservatory, Bellagio** > p.49. Part greenhouse, part camp and colourful fantasyland, Bellagio's indoor flower show must be seen to be believed.

3 **Eiffel Tower Experience** > p.57. Ride into the skies atop Las Vegas's own miniature version of Paris and look down on the rest of the Strip.

🍴 **Lunch** > p.64. Enjoy a quintessentially French bistro meal, with a ringside seat on the Strip, at *Mon Ami Gabi* in Paris.

4 **The Forum Shops** > p.62. Marble statues, fountains and a false sky that cycles hourly between day and night; is it ancient Rome or simply Caesars Palace?

5 **Grand Canal Shoppes** > p.77. Operatic gondoliers ply the waters of the Grand Canal, serenading shoppers perusing the Venetian's upstairs, upmarket mall.

🍴 **Dinner** > p.81. Pan-Asian food and lush red decor at *Wazuzu* in Wynn Las Vegas combine to offer a memorable dining experience.

6 **Love, the Mirage** > p.84. Las Vegas's favourite Canadian clowns, the Cirque du Soleil, join forces with the Beatles to stunning effect.

7 **Omnia, Caesars Palace** > p.66. Experience Las Vegas's new breed of breathtaking clubs at Caesars' showpiece indoor-outdoor *Omnia*.

Day Two in Las Vegas

1 **Il Fornaio, New York–New York** > p.40. This New York-style Italian bakery is the perfect place to grab breakfast.

2 **The Big Apple Coaster, New York–New York** > p.36. Let's shake things up – loop around the Manhattan skyline in a little yellow cab, upside down, at 70mph.

3 **Excalibur** > p.34. If things haven't been kitsch enough yet, stroll through this bizarre Arthurian castle-casino.

4 **Luxor** > p.33. Things are getting weirder – enter an Egyptian pyramid through the paws of the Sphinx to see artefacts recovered from the *Titanic*.

5 **Shark Reef, Mandalay Bay** > p.31. Watch crocodiles and sharks swim amid the ruins of a Mayan temple.

Lunch > p.39. Break for a Mexican meal beside Mandalay Bay's wave pool, at the *Border Grill*.

6 **CSI The Experience, MGM Grand** > p.37. After lunch use your razor-sharp forensic skills to solve a murder.

7 **Art collection, CityCenter** > p.47. Standing aloof from the Strip, the sleek, modernist CityCenter district holds a surprising array of contemporary sculptures from the likes of Maya Lin, Henry Moore and Antony Gormley.

8 **The Shops at Crystals** > p.50. The flamboyant interior of Las Vegas's priciest mall is well worth seeing.

Dinner > p.52. Dine on superb "new Italian" food in *Scarpetta*, overlooking Bellagio's fountains.

9 **Britney Spears** > p.67. See the definitive twenty-first-century headliner deliver a song-and-dance show in the finest Las Vegas tradition.

Classic Las Vegas

For those who yearn for the days when casinos smelled of mobster menace and the Rat Pack ruled the Strip, the new, corporate-owned Las Vegas can sometimes feel too tasteful for comfort. Vestiges of the bad old days still survive, though, if you know where to look.

1 The Flamingo > p.60. Okay, so the Flamingo these days is more Donny Osmond than Bugsy Siegel, but the original Strip resort still holds plenty of classic kitsch, including its trademark pink flamingoes.

2 Caesars Palace > p.58. With its half-naked centurions and Cleopatras, Caesars is where the Strip first veered towards full-on fantasy fifty years ago – and it hasn't let up since.

Lunch > p.91. The all-you-can-eat buffet is one tradition Las Vegas will never let go; prices have risen on the Strip, but head downtown and you'll find amazing value, at the *Paradise Buffet*, for example.

3 The Mob Museum > p.90. There's no better place to learn the seedy story of Las Vegas's shady past than at this gripping, gruesome museum downtown.

4 El Cortez > p.89. For the true Las Vegas experience, gamble in downtown's least-changed casino, with its hard-bitten characters and rock-bottom odds.

5 Fremont Street Experience > p.86. All bright lights and flashing neon, downtown's must-see block-spanning canopy is pure old-fashioned spectacle.

Dinner > p.92. Former mayor Oscar Goodman's steakhouse, *Oscar's Beef * Booze * Broads*, oozes unabashed love for downtown's long-lost heyday.

6 Peppermill Fireside Lounge > p.82. Round things off with a nightcap martini in this flamboyant round-the-clock Stripside relic.

Budget Las Vegas

While Las Vegas is not the budget destination it used to be, it's still possible to visit on the cheap if you play your cards right (better still, don't play cards at all…).

1 Excalibur > p.116. Wake up in your "wide-screen" room at Excalibur – from $50 for a large suite, they're the Strip's best value.

2 Free monorails > p.126. Hop on the free monorail system to see Luxor and Mandalay Bay.

3 The Deuce > p.125. Ride the Deuce bus north from Mandalay Bay and enjoy the Strip in all its glory.

4 The Midway > p.75. Stop off at Circus Circus to watch free circus performances on the Midway stage.

Lunch > p.62. Head for Caesars Palace and buy a "Buffet of Buffets" pass, valid for 24 hours at all Caesars' properties. Start with the *Bacchanal Buffet*, which epitomizes decadent Las Vegas excess.

5 Mac King > p.67. Cross the Strip to Harrah's to enjoy the best-value show in town – the clownish, endearing Mac King and his family-fun comedy magic.

6 Big Elvis > p.66. Simply stay in Harrah's and head for the no-cover Piano Bar, where the hunka-hunka love that is Pete Vallee keeps on burning all afternoon.

7 The Volcano > p.69. Once darkness falls, take your place outside the Mirage and watch the volcano erupt.

Dinner > p.62. Use your "Buffet of Buffets" pass again to sample the irresistible selection of all-French cuisine at *Le Village Buffet* in Paris.

8 Bellagio Fountains > p.49. The mesmerizing jets of this free water ballet make a suitably soothing end to the day.

Big sights

1 The Venetian Festooned with dazzling frescoes and echoing to the song of costumed gondoliers, the opulent Venetian is loved by kids, clubbers and culture vultures alike. > **p.71**

2 Bellagio Las Vegas at its most luxurious, an Italianate marble extravaganza with its own eight-acre lake. > **p.48**

4 Hoover Dam A mighty wall of concrete holding back the Colorado River – the architectural showpiece that made Las Vegas possible. > **p.106**

3 Fremont Street Experience Where else has the sheer chutzpah to roof over four entire city blocks just so they can project multicoloured snakes and aliens onto the ceiling? > **p.86**

5 Caesars Palace This huge and ever-playful casino is a city in itself – and an ancient Roman one at that. > **p.58**

Shows

1 **Kà** For sheer spectacle and breathtaking stunts, the most jaw-dropping Cirque show in town. > **p.43**

2 Terry Fator
Old-fashioned family entertainment, taken to another dimension thanks to ventriloquist Fator's uncanny singing skills. > **p.85**

3 Blue Man Group A bizarre but compelling blend of performance art, slapstick and high-octane rock. > **p.42**

4 Love Cirque meets the Beatles, in a double whammy of music and performance. > **p.84**

5 Human Nature
Four likeable Aussies pay harmonious homage to the fabulous Motown sound. > **p.84**

Restaurants

1 Bouchon, the Venetian The menu at Thomas Keller's French bistro is every bit as special as the setting, on an elegant upper-storey patio. **> p.78**

2 Mon Ami Gabi, Paris The perfect venue for an al fresco French lunch, on a pavement patio beneath Paris's Eiffel Tower. > **p.64**

3 Beijing Noodle No. 9, Caesars Dazzling futuristic decor makes this mid-priced pan-Asian diner a truly memorable experience. > **p.63**

4 Scarpetta, Cosmopolitan Watch the Bellagio fountains as you savour Scott Conant's wonderful contemporary take on Italian cuisine. > **p.52**

5 Jean Philippe Patisserie, Bellagio Pastries and drinks to die for, given an extra air of indulgence by the extraordinary, swirling chocolate fountain. > **p.51**

Offbeat exhibits

1 Titanic: The Artifact Exhibition The world's only permanent display of *Titanic* artefacts, including a huge and very eerie chunk of the ship herself, upstairs in the Luxor pyramid. > **p.33**

2 The Mob Museum
Downtown's prestigious new museum tells the story of the men who made Las Vegas – and the men who arrested them. **> p.90**

3 Secret Garden and Dolphin Habitat Siegfried and Roy are long gone from the Mirage, but their famed white tigers (and lions) are still prowling the gardens. **> p.69**

4 Bodies...the Exhibition What better place to look for dead bodies than a gigantic pyramid? Luxor makes an obvious home for this gruesome but uplifting exhibit. **> p.34**

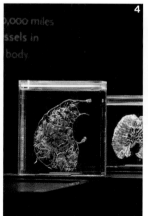

5 CSI: The Experience A hugely enjoyable interactive adventure, in which visitors can test their wits to solve a mysterious recent murder. **> p.37**

Shopping

1 Miracle Mile Shops With larger stores, and more of them, the best Strip mall for leisurely browsing and shopping around. > **p.62**

2 Grand Canal Shoppes As much for souvenir hunters and sightseers as serious shoppers, the Venetian's Grand Canal is a great place for window shopping. > **p.77**

4 The Forum Shops America's most profitable shopping mall, stuffed inside the faux-Roman pomp of Caesars Palace – though the price tags are real enough. > **p.62**

3 Fashion Show The one Strip mall not linked to a casino offers large department stores as well as designer boutiques, across from Wynn Las Vegas. > **p.77**

5 Town Square At the far southern end of the Strip, this locals' favourite is not so much a mall as an outdoor shopping neighbourhood. > **p.38**

Thrill rides

1 **The Big Apple Coaster** Climb aboard a tiny yellow taxi-cab and loop the loop around New York–New York. > **p.36**

2 **Dig This!** If you've always wanted to drive a bulldozer, or play basketball with a giant digger, this is where your dreams come true. > **p.94**

4 **Stratosphere Thrill Rides** The craziest thrill rides of all – spin off the Stratosphere strapped to a lurching bench or simply jump off the edge. > **p.76**

3 **SlotZilla** Zip lines are the new big thing in Las Vegas, this one lets you slide the length of the Fremont Street Experience. > **p.87**

5 **Las Vegas High Roller** The world's biggest observation wheel, 550ft high, commands tremendous views over the city. > **p.61**

The deserts

1 Zion National Park You can drive to Utah's magnificent red-rock park in little more than two hours to enjoy dramatic scenery and breathtaking hikes. > **p.110**

2 Valley of Fire Luric desert scenery, bizarre rock formations and supremely remote hiking. > **p.107**

3 Grand Canyon South Rim Seeing Arizona's world-famous wonder makes a fabulous weekend road trip, but you can also fly there and back in a day. > **p.109**

4 Red Rock Canyon Las Vegas's great escape; hike and bike amid stunning red-rock sandscapes just twenty miles from the Strip. > **p.104**

5 Grand Canyon West Venture out onto the Skywalk or take a helicopter ride down to the Colorado River; the West Rim is a pricey day-trip by air, but you won't forget the adventure. > **p.108**

27

PLACES

The South Strip

For seven decades huge casinos have pushed ever further south along Las Vegas Boulevard, and what constitutes the South Strip has been repeatedly redefined. One thing has remained constant, however: entrepreneurs love to build lavish, eye-catching properties here because they're the first to be seen by drivers arriving from southern California. The current generation thus includes a scale model of Manhattan, New York–New York; the vast MGM Grand; a fantasy castle, Excalibur; an Egyptian pyramid, Luxor; and what's currently the true start of the Strip, the gleaming tropical paradise of Mandalay Bay. Thanks to successive buyouts and mergers, all these five are now owned by MGM Resorts and run as a cohesive unit. The exception, the ageing Tropicana, has, not surprisingly, struggled to keep up.

MANDALAY BAY

3950 Las Vegas Blvd S ☎ 877 632 7700, ⓦ mandalaybay.com. MAP P.32, POCKET MAP B7

The southernmost mega-casino on the Strip, **Mandalay Bay**, consists of two golden skyscrapers that tower over a sprawling complex covering a greater area than any other single property in Las Vegas. Linked to Luxor (see p.33) and Excalibur (p.34) by a stand-alone outdoor **monorail** as well as indoor walkways, it belongs to the same owners, MGM Resorts. It was built in 1999 to provide a more sophisticated alternative to what were then its more overtly child-oriented neighbours, and apart from the **Shark Reef** aquarium (see p.31) offers little to lure in casual sightseers.

MANDALAY BAY

"Welcome to Fabulous Las Vegas"

Familiar no doubt from every Las Vegas movie or TV show you've ever seen, the "Welcome to Fabulous Las Vegas" sign is an obligatory photo op for every visitor, just over half a mile south of Mandalay Bay. To minimize the risk of accidents, only cars heading south, away from the city, can access the narrow patch in between the north- and southbound carriageways of the Strip. Don't try walking this far, least of all in summer.

Beyond a certain vague tropical theming, there's no significance to the name "Mandalay". Instead Mandalay Bay's strongest selling point is its nightlife, with a high-end array of restaurants, bars, clubs – such as *Light* (p.42), the first-ever nightclub to be run under the auspices of Cirque du Soleil – and music venues, including the prestigious *House of Blues* (p.42), plus the self-explanatory Cirque show, *Michael Jackson One*. To keep its young, affluent guests on site during the day as well, there's also an impressively landscaped network of pools and artificial beaches that includes a wave pool and the "toptional" **Moorea Beach Club**.

Being further south of the Strip's centre of gravity than anyone would choose to walk, Mandalay Bay can feel a little stranded. Forced to work hard to attract and keep visitors, however, it has continued to prosper through the recession. Inevitably, some of its restaurants have lost their original buzz, while the Mandalay Place mall holds little to lure shoppers based elsewhere. For a night out, though, or a weekend in a self-contained luxury resort, Mandalay Bay can still match the best Las Vegas has to offer.

Incidentally, the *Four Seasons* hotel is right here too – its rooms occupy the top five floors of Mandalay Bay's original tower.

SHARK REEF

Mandalay Bay, 3950 Las Vegas Blvd ☎ 702 632 4555, ⓦ sharkreef.com. June–Aug daily 10am–10pm; Sept–May Mon–Thurs & Sun 10am–8pm, Fr & Sat 10am–10pm Ages 13 and over $20, ages 4–12 $14. MAP P.32, POCKET MAP B8

In keeping with Las Vegas's emphasis on immediate thrills, the **Shark Reef** aquarium focuses almost exclusively on dangerous marine predators, prowling through tanks designed to resemble a decaying ancient temple that's sinking into the sea. The species on show – largely chosen for their scary teeth and deadly stings – include giant crocodiles and Komodo dragons, as well, of course, as enormous sharks. Separate eerily illuminated cylindrical tanks are filled with menacing-looking jellyfish.

Shark Reef is located right at the back of Mandalay Bay; to reach it, you have to walk along several hundred yards of internal corridors, beyond the two convention centres.

SHARK REEF

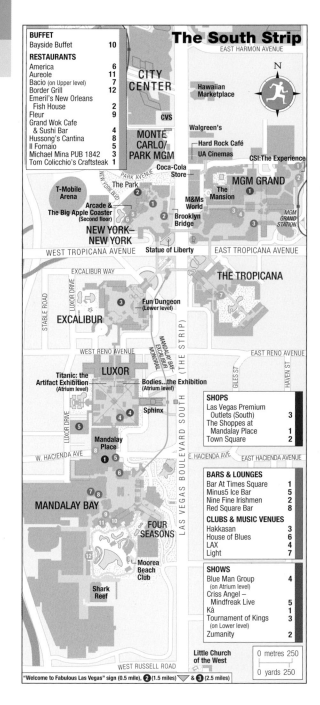

The South Strip

BUFFET
Bayside Buffet — 10

RESTAURANTS
America — 6
Aureole — 11
Bacio (on Upper level) — 7
Border Grill — 12
Emeril's New Orleans
 Fish House — 2
Fleur — 9
Grand Wok Cafe
 & Sushi Bar — 4
Hussong's Cantina — 8
Il Fornaio — 5
Michael Mina PUB 1842 — 3
Tom Colicchio's Craftsteak — 1

EAST HARMON AVENUE
CITY CENTER
Hawaiian Marketplace
CVS
Walgreen's
MONTE CARLO/ PARK MGM
Hard Rock Café
UA Cinemas
CSI:The Experience
PARK AVENUE
Coca-Cola Store
The Park
MGM GRAND
NEW YORK BLVD
T-Mobile Arena
The Mansion
M&Ms World
Arcade & The Big Apple Coaster (Second floor)
Brooklyn Bridge
MGM GRAND STATION
NEW YORK– NEW YORK
Statue of Liberty
WEST TROPICANA AVENUE
EAST TROPICANA AVENUE
EXCALIBUR WAY
THE TROPICANA
EXCALIBUR DRIVE
Fun Dungeon (Lower level)
STABLE ROAD
EXCALIBUR
WEST RENO AVENUE
EAST RENO AVENUE
GILES ST
HAVEN ST
LUXOR
MANDALAY BAY EXCALIBUR MONORAIL
(THE STRIP)
Titanic: the Artifact Exhibition (Atrium level)
Bodies...the Exhibition (Atrium level)
LUXOR DRIVE
Sphinx
LAS VEGAS BOULEVARD SOUTH
Mandalay Place
W. HACIENDA AVE
E. HACIENDA AVE
EAST HACIENDA AVENUE
MANDALAY BAY
FOUR SEASONS
Moorea Beach Club
Shark Reef
WEST RUSSELL ROAD

SHOPS
Las Vegas Premium
 Outlets (South) — 3
The Shoppes at
 Mandalay Place — 1
Town Square — 2

BARS & LOUNGES
Bar At Times Square — 1
Minus5 Ice Bar — 5
Nine Fine Irishmen — 2
Red Square Bar — 8

CLUBS & MUSIC VENUES
Hakkasan — 3
House of Blues — 6
LAX — 4
Light — 7

SHOWS
Blue Man Group — 4
 (on Atrium level)
Criss Angel –
 Mindfreak Live — 5
Kà — 1
Tournament of Kings — 3
 (on Lower level)
Zumanity — 2

Little Church of the West

0 metres 250
0 yards 250

"Welcome to Fabulous Las Vegas" sign (0.5 mile), ② (1.5 miles) ▽ & ③ (2.5 miles)

LUXOR

3900 Las Vegas Blvd S ☎702 262 4444,
Ⓦluxor.com. MAP P.32, POCKET MAP B6

The huge **Luxor** pyramid, with
its sloping, monolithic walls of
black shiny glass, was built in
1993 as the follow-up to the
much more fanciful Excalibur
(see p.34) next door. Originally
it was filled to bursting with
ancient Egyptian motifs,
holding not only a replica of
King Tut's tomb but even an
indoor River Nile. Then, when
Las Vegas (and owners MGM
Resorts in particular) decided to
gear itself less towards kids and
more towards adults, much of
Luxor's archeological theming
was stripped away. Nothing can
mask the fact that it's a colossal
pyramid, though, and Luxor
today seems to be in an odd sort
of limbo, embarrassed about its
Egyptian past but unable to find
an alternative identity.

Visitors who venture this far
down the Strip – especially those
arriving on the **Mandalay
Bay–Excalibur monorail** – still
congregate outside to take
photos of the enormous Sphinx
that straddles the main driveway.
Immediately inside the main
doors, there's also a re-creation
of the facade of the Egyptian
temple of Abu Simbel. Beyond
that, however, there's little to
distinguish the main casino
floor. In the absence of
noteworthy restaurants or shops,
Luxor is best known for its bars
and clubs, including an outpost
of LA stalwart *LAX* (see p.42).

Immediately upstairs, the
so-called Atrium Level is
home to two permanent
exhibitions – **Bodies** (see p.34)
and **Titanic** – as well as a small
food court. It's also the best
vantage point from which to
admire the pyramid's cavernous
interior; only guests can access
the higher levels.

LUXOR

TITANIC: THE ARTIFACT EXHIBITION

Atrium Level, Luxor, 3900 Las Vegas Blvd S
☎702 262 4400, Ⓦrmstitanic.net. Daily
10am–10pm. $32, ages 4–12 $24, over-64s
$30; audio guides $6 extra. MAP P.32,
POCKET MAP A6

Held in an enclosed building
upstairs in Luxor, **Titanic:
The Artifact Exhibition** is
the world's only permanent
exhibition of items salvaged
from the *Titanic*. Displays
that also include mock-ups
of the fabled Grand Staircase
tell the full story of the great
ship, from construction to
destruction. Each visitor is
invited to pose for a souvenir
photo on the Staircase, and as
you enter you receive a
"boarding pass" named for
a specific passenger. Only as
you leave do you find out
whether he or she survived
the catastrophe.

Prize artefacts include the
actual wheel at which the
helmsman tried and failed to
steer clear of the iceberg on
April 14, 1912, and the
enormous Big Piece, a
gigantic slab that broke off
C Deck as the ship sank, and
which was raised from the
ocean floor in 1998.

BODIES...THE EXHIBITION

Atrium Level, Luxor, 3900 Las Vegas Blvd S
☎ 702 262 4400, ⓦ bodiestheexhibition.com.
Daily 10am–10pm, last admission 9pm. $32,
ages 4–12 $24, over-64s $30; audio guides $6
extra. MAP P.32, POCKET MAP A5

You might expect **Bodies...the
Exhibition** to be a gory horror
show. In fact, despite the
advertising images of goggle-
eyed corpses, it provides a
surprisingly serious museum-
quality experience. You have to
keep reminding yourself that
what look like brightly coloured
mannequins really are dead
bodies that have been
"plastinated" for permanent
display. Some are posed as
though in life, playing sports in
perpetuity, others have been
dissected to show particular
features of their anatomy.
Certain sections, like that in
which an entire circulatory
system, down to the tiniest
capillary, has been teased out
and dyed in different colours,
have an astonishing beauty; the
sight of fatally diseased organs
displayed alongside healthy
counterparts are much more
sobering. Even if you've
wandered in for a quick laugh,
you may leave determined to
change your life around – not
that Las Vegas is necessarily the
best place to start.

EXCALIBUR

3850 Las Vegas Blvd S ☎ 702 597 7777,
ⓦ excalibur.com. MAP P.32, POCKET MAP B4

Built in 1990, **Excalibur**
remains the most visible
reminder of the era when Las
Vegas briefly reinvented itself
as a vast children's playground.
With its jam-packed, multicoloured turrets and ring of
clunky battlements it doesn't so
much look like a castle, as like
a child's drawing of a castle –
and to be more specific still,
a drawing of Walt Disney's
version of Sleeping Beauty's
castle. In fact, the architect
responsible, Veldon Simpson,
who later went on to design
both Luxor and the MGM
Grand, had travelled around
Europe visiting hundreds of
real-life castles. He ultimately
settled on using the same model
that Disney had, Neuschwan-
stein in Bavaria, a whimsical
hybrid of French château and
stern German fortress. Only a
nit-picker would mention that
the original Excalibur was a
sword, not a castle.

These days, Excalibur is less
child-oriented than it used to
be. Its primary function for
current owners MGM seems to
be as a kind of gateway to draw
visitors towards the southern
end of the Strip, complementing

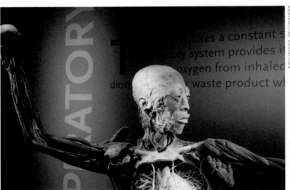

BODIES...THE EXHIBITION

the free monorail to Luxor (see p.33) and Mandalay Bay (p.30), prominent outside, with an easy indoor walkway to those properties further back. You access that by heading onto the upper level from the casino, lured ever onwards along the corridor by boutiques and fast-food places.

As Excalibur generally offers some of the Strip's least expensive hotel rooms, it caters largely to low-budget tour groups and families. That can result in a slightly jarring clash between its remaining child-friendly Arthurian theming, which includes the jousting-and-serving-wenches dinner-show *Tournament of Kings* (see p.43), and blue-collar adult entertainment such as *Dick's Last Resort* bar and the *Thunder From Down Under* male stripper revue. Its lowest level, below the casino floor, is occupied by the **Fun Dungeon** (daily 10am–10pm), a jumble of fairground stalls, carnival amusements and arcade games.

Much of the upstairs, officially known as the Castle Walk Level, is taken up by a huge **food court**, which includes a massive *Krispy Kreme* doughnut bakery, where all the kitchen action is open to passers-by, and a *Tropical Smoothie Café* outlet. It's also home to the frankly poor *Excalibur Buffet* and assorted souvenir "shoppes".

THE TROPICANA

3801 Las Vegas Blvd S ⓣ 702 739 2222, ⓦ www.troplv.com. MAP P.32 POCKET MAP C4

Built in 1957, and standing proudly aloof a mile south of the Strip, the **Tropicana** swiftly became a byword for luxury. It was also renowned from the start as being in the pocket of the Mob, and spent twenty years under investigation for the "skimming" of casino profits, money laundering and other Mafia-related skulduggery.

THE TROPICANA

Although it's now poised at the country's busiest crossroads, the Tropicana has long struggled to compete with its mighty MGM-owned neighbours – Excalibur (p.34), the MGM Grand (p.37), and New York–New York (p.36). Barely rescued from bankruptcy in 2008, it was given a $125-million makeover intended to restore its tropical-playground image and add something of the feel of Miami's South Beach. Among the casualties of that process was its fabled topless revue, the Folies Bergere, which sadly ended its residency shortly before its fiftieth anniversary.

While it's looking much crisper and brighter than before, the Tropicana still can't match the latest Strip giants. Hopes that it would blossom as a nightlife destination have failed to materialize, and it holds little to draw in sightseers, shoppers or diners. Instead it remains slightly apart, with its strongest feature being an extensive pool complex that's open to guests only.

NEW YORK–NEW YORK

NEW YORK–NEW YORK

3790 Las Vegas Blvd S ☏ 702 740 6969, ⓦ newyorknewyork.com. MAP P.32, POCKET MAP B3

The first, and arguably the best, of Las Vegas's modern breed of replica "cities", **New York–New York** opened in 1997. Its exterior consists of a squeezed-up, half-sized rendition of the Manhattan skyline as it looked in the 1950s. The interior, which makes no attempt to correspond to the specific "buildings" outside, holds a smaller than average casino, plus a dining and nightlife district intended to evoke Greenwich Village.

Despite the broad Brooklyn Bridge that stretches along the Strip sidewalk, and the Empire State and Chrysler buildings etched against the Nevada sky, the most iconic feature of the facade is the **Statue of Liberty**, facing the intersection with Tropicana Avenue. Unlike the other elements here it's actually twice the height of the real-life statue. This spot never hosted a replica of the World Trade Center, but ad hoc memorials appeared here after September 11, 2001.

New York–New York has lost much of its original playful theming in recent years.

Sightseers once stepped off the Strip to find themselves in Central Park at night, with owls peeping down from the trees. Things are more serious these days, enlivened here and there with stylish Art Deco motifs.

New York–New York isn't served by any monorail, but pedestrians pass through one corner en route between the pedestrian bridges to Excalibur and the MGM Grand. Perhaps to tempt them to stay, the areas nearest the Strip hold an abundance of bars, pubs and food outlets. Much of the second floor is taken up by the Arcade, a rather ramshackle assortment of sideshows, games and kids' attractions.

THE BIG APPLE COASTER

New York–New York, 3790 Las Vegas Blvd S ☏ 702 740 6616, ⓦ newyorknewyork.com. Daily 10.30am–midnight. $14 first ride, $25 for an all-day Scream Pass. MAP P.32, POCKET MAP B3

From the moment you catch a glimpse of New York–New York, you'll almost certainly also see – and hear – the tiny little yellow cabs that loop and race around its skyscraper towers. Previously known first as the Manhattan Express, then simply as The Roller Coaster, and now re-renamed **The Big Apple Coaster**, it operates from a replica subway station on the casino's upper floor. Speeding at 67mph, plunging over 200ft and rolling like a jet fighter, it's a serious thrill ride no theme-park fan should miss.

MGM GRAND

3799 Las Vegas Blvd S ☏ £77 880 0680, ⓦ mgmgrand.com. MAP P.32, POCKET MAP C3

The enormous **MGM Grand** casino has been through many changes since it opened in 1993. Back then, it attracted huge publicity as the largest hotel in the world and the first to incorporate its own theme park. It was also the location of the legendary 1997 boxing fight during which Mike Tyson bit Evander Holyfield's ear.

These days, however, the MGM Grand keeps a lower profile, and it would be hard to say quite what identity it's aiming for any more. All traces of the theme park have long since vanished, while only the general preponderance of green now recalls the property's initial *Wizard of Oz* theme. With its original 5005 rooms boosted by the addition of the three all-suite *Signature* towers, it's surpassed in size only by the Venetian-Palazzo combination. Only in Las Vegas could such a behemoth seem to blend into the background.

One reason for this may be that with so many guests on site, the MGM Grand simply doesn't need to lure visitors in. It still boasts a fabulous array of dining and entertainment options, which includes the stunning Cirque de Soleil show *Kà*, and the *Joël Robuchon Restaurant*, where the $425 Degustation Menu is said to be the world's most expensive prix fixe menu.

Over the last few years, MGM Resorts have undertaken a massive overhaul of the Grand that has so far seen more old things disappear than new ones emerge. Casualties have included the live lions previously displayed in a glass enclosure just off the Strip, and the veteran *Studio 54* nightclub.

CSI: THE EXPERIENCE

MGM Grand 3799 Las Vegas Blvd S ☏ 702 891 5749, ⓦ csiexhibit.com. Daily 9am–9pm, last admission 8pm. Ages 12 and over $28, $26 for repeat visits on same day, ages 4–11 $21/$20. MAP P.32, POCKET MAP E2

Set well back from the MGM Grand's Strip entrance, **CSI: The Experience** is perhaps the most enjoyable family attraction in Las Vegas. Trading on the worldwide success of the CSI TV franchise, it enables participants to investigate, and almost certainly solve, fictional murder mysteries.

Each ticket entitles you to solve one of three possible cases, taking roughly an hour to examine the murder scene, test out various hypotheses in the lab, and come up with a solution. Assistants are on hand to help, though you don't interact with any actors.

CSI: THE EXPERIENCE

Shops

LAS VEGAS PREMIUM OUTLETS (SOUTH)

7400 Las Vegas Blvd S ☎ 702 896 5599, ⓦ premiumoutlets.com. Mon–Sat 9am–9pm, Sun 9am–8pm. MAP P.32 & P.95, POCKET MAP B13

The sort of mall you might find beside the highway on the outskirts of any town in America, Las Vegas Premium Outlets (South), 3 miles south of Mandalay Bay, offers no-frills, no-nonsense shopping at Banana Republic, Gap, Nike and the like. For visitors with the use of a car, it's not a bad option for picking up everyday items to take back home. There's a basic fast-food court but no restaurants.

THE SHOPPES AT MANDALAY PLACE

Mandalay Bay, 3930 Las Vegas Blvd S ☎ 702 632 7777, ⓦ mandalaybay.com. Daily 10am–11pm; hours for individual stores may vary. MAP P.32, POCKET MAP B6

Arranged along the indoor hallway that connects Mandalay Bay with Luxor – a fair walk from the centre of either, and from the monorail too – The Shoppes at Mandalay Place does not rank among Las Vegas's premier shopping malls. Instead, it's a rather haphazard mix of big names such as The Guinness Store, Nike Golf and Swarovski, and smart boutiques, galleries and novelty stores, plus several bars and restaurants.

TOWN SQUARE

6605 Las Vegas Blvd S ☎ 702 269 5001, ⓦ mytownsquarelasvegas.com. Mon–Thurs 10am–9pm, Fri & Sat 10am–10pm, Sun 11am–8pm. MAP P.32 & P.95, POCKET MAP B13

Especially popular with locals who prefer to steer clear of the Strip, Town Square, 3 miles south of Mandalay Bay, is a rarity in Las Vegas, designed to be experienced as an outdoor "neighbourhood" rather than an air-conditioned enclave. Visitors from further afield may be less enthused by its attempt to evoke the feel of a "European village". Big stores include Staples, a Whole Foods supermarket and an Apple Store that offers free wi-fi; there are also some unremarkable restaurants and a cinema.

Buffet

BAYSIDE BUFFET

Mandalay Bay, 3950 Las Vegas Blvd S ☎ 702 632 7402, ⓦ mandalaybay.com. Mon–Fri 7–11am $18, 11am–2.30pm $22, 4.45–9.45pm $33; Sat & Sun 7am–2.30pm $26 & 4.45–9.45pm $35. MAP P.32, POCKET MAP B7

Mandalay Bay's buffet has a much nicer setting than most of its Las Vegas rivals, overlooking the resort's pool, and open, when weather permits, to breezes. Apart from the wide range of desserts, though, and the pre-cut deli sandwiches at lunchtime, the food is not all that amazing.

MANDALAY BAY

Restaurants

AMERICA

New York–New York, 3790 Las Vegas Blvd S 702 740 6451, newyorknewyork.com. Daily 24hr. MAP P.32, POCKET MAP B3

While serious foodies will find nothing remarkable about this 24-hour diner, it's a great place to bring kids, or Las Vegas first-timers, thanks to the colossal, cartoon-like relief map of the USA that hangs from the ceiling. Serving signature dishes from all over the country, from Alaskan salmon salad ($16) to Kansas City ribs ($25), there's food to match every appetite.

AUREOLE

Mandalay Bay, 3950 Las Vegas Blvd S 702 632 7200, aureolelv.com. Mon-Sat 5.30–10.30pm. MAP P.32, POCKET MAP B7

With its astonishing "wine tower", a 42ft vertical wine cellar that's accessed by flying, white-clad "wine angels", Chef Charlie Palmer's showcase restaurant is a real must-see. His contemporary American cooking is something special, with the menu divided into "Root", "Ranch" and "Surf". The filet mignon entrée costs $59, while baked salmon is $31.

BACIO

Tropicana, 3801 Las Vegas Blvd S 800 462 8767, troplv.com. Daily 5–10pm. MAP P.32, POCKET MAP C4

Carla Pellegrino's classic Italian diner has been a big hit at the revamped Tropicana, not least for its dazzling bright-white styling. The speciality veal chop costs over $40, but you can get fresh pasta with marinara sauce for $22, and the early-evening set tasting menu offers four courses with wine for $39. The one drawback is the occasionally slow service.

BORDER GRILL

Mandalay Bay, 3950 Las Vegas Blvd S 702 632 7403, bordergrill.com. Mon-Thurs 11am–10pm, Fri 11am–11pm, Sat 10am–11pm, Sun 10am–10pm. MAP P.32, POCKET MAP B3

Serving light and zestful "modern Mexican" cuisine that's a perfect match for its sun-kissed indoor-outdoor setting, this poolside veteran serves lunchtime salads, tacos and *tortas* (flatbreads) for well under $20, and larger dinner plates like Yucatan pork for $24 or *mole* roasted chicken for $28. A three-course set dinner costs $42 and the hugely popular weekend brunch $35.

EMERIL'S NEW ORLEANS FISH HOUSE

MGM Grand, 3799 Las Vegas Blvd S 702 891 7374, emerils.com. Daily 11.30am–10pm. MAP P.32, POCKET MAP E2

Rich New Orleans flavours in a modern setting, courtesy of TV chef Emeril Lagasse. As the name suggests, the emphasis is on seafood, with barbecue shrimp as an appetizer ($17) and pecan-crusted redfish as a main course ($37), but you can also get seared chicken or a rib-eye steak. If you don't have a dinner reservation, they should be able to seat you after 9pm.

FLEUR

Mandalay Bay, 3950 Las Vegas Blvd S ☎702 632 7200, ⓦ mandalaybay.com. Mon–Fri 11am–10pm, Sat & Sun 11am–10.30pm. MAP P.32, POCKET MAP B7

There's much more to Hubert Keller's modern tapas restaurant than its notorious $5000 foie gras burger. Its sumptuous menu features exquisite dishes from all over the world, including Spanish-style grilled octopus ($22) and Greek herb-roasted leg of lamb ($48). Even the so-called "Large Plates" are pretty small, though, so it's no place to be counting your pennies. Parties of four can "Tour the World" for $310.

GRAND WOK & SUSHI BAR

MGM Grand, 3799 Las Vegas Blvd S ☎702 891 7433, ⓦ mgmgrand.com. Mon–Thurs & Sun 11am–10pm, Fri & Sat 11am–midnight. No reservations. MAP P.32, POCKET MAP D3

This pan-Asian restaurant is the kind of place you wish you could find everywhere in Las Vegas. The prices are low, the service fast, the decor fancy enough to make you feel you're somewhere special and they only take walk-ins. And the food? That's great too, drawing on Vietnamese, Thai, Chinese and Japanese. Dim sum and sushi plates cost around $12, and mains more like $20.

HUSSONG'S CANTINA

Mandalay Bay, 3930 Las Vegas Blvd S ☎702 632 6450, ⓦ hussongslasvegas.com. Mon–Thurs & Sun 11am–10pm, Fri & Sat 11am–11pm. MAP P.32, POCKET MAP B6

An outpost of the Mexican original that's said to have invented the margarita, *Hussong's* is as much a bar as a restaurant. Yet the food itself is surprisingly good, with $15–20 flautas, fajitas and chimichangas, and $14 nachos. Don't miss the $6 plazero corn, which is dusted with cheese flakes.

IL FORNAIO

New York–New York, 3790 Las Vegas Blvd S ☎702 650 6500, ⓦ ilfornaio.com/lasvegas. Restaurant Mon–Thurs & Sun 7.30am–11pm, Fri & Sat 7.30am–midnight; Panetteria daily 6am–5.30pm. MAP P.32, POCKET MAP B3

While *Il Fornaio* is open for decent Italian food pretty much round the clock, in-the-know locals love it best of all in the morning, when you can enjoy a wonderful sit-down breakfast or simply pop in to the separate deli/bakery next door for fresh breads and espresso coffee.

MICHAEL MINA PUB 1842

MGM Grand, 3799 Las Vegas Blvd S ☎702 891 3922, ⓦ mgmgrand.com. Mon–Thurs 11.30am–10pm, Fri & Sat 11.30am–11pm, Sun 10am–10pm. MAP P.32, POCKET MAP D3

Top Las Vegas chef Michael Mina keeps things simple with his take on the gastro pub, serving substantial $18–22 burgers and old-fashioned favourites like fish and chips ($26) or succulent St Louis ribs ($22/34), along with $8–11 Happy Hour "small plates" like brisket sliders or lobster grilled cheese and a couple of dozen draught beers.

IL FORNAIO

TOM COLICCHIO'S CRAFTSTEAK

MGM Grand, 3799 Las Vegas Elvd S ☎ 702 891 7318, ⓦ craftsteaklasvegas.com. Mon–Thurs & Sun 5–10pm, Fri & Sat 5–10.30pm. MAP P.32, POCKET MAP E2

Serious carnivores swear this dinner-only steakhouse serves the best beef in Las Vegas, in melt-in-your-mouth inch-thick cuts. Order à la cart; there's lobster bisque ($19) as an appetizer and steaks from $38. Set menus range from $125 for domestic Angus beef to $275 for Wagyu surf & turf.

Bars and lounges

BAR AT TIMES SQUARE

New York–New York, 3790 Las Vegas Blvd S ☎ 702 740 6466, ⓦ newyorknewyork.com. Mon–Thurs 1pm–2am, Fri–Sun 11am–2.30am, showtime 8pm–2am. Cover $10 standing, reserved seating Mon–Thurs & Sun $15, Fri & Sat $25. MAP P.32, POCKET MAP B3

If you like your nights out sophisticated or edgy, steer clear of this raucous sing-a-long bar alongside New York–New York's main casino floor; if you prefer to scream along at the top of your voice as two pianists go head-to-head, playing whatever requests spring to their tipsy audience's mind, you're in the right place.

MINUS5 ICE BAR

Mandalay Bay, 3930 Las Vegas Blvd S ☎ 702 740 5800, ⓦ www.minus5experience.com. Mon–Thurs & Sun 11am–2am, Fri & Sat 11am–3am. Cover varies, typically $25 including one drink. MAP P.32, POCKET MAP B6

This funny, gimmicky bar is exactly what it says it is – everything is made of ice, from walls to glasses (though the couches are spread with deer skins). Customers are loaned jackets, gloves and boots to tolerate the minus 5 temperature.

MINUS5 ICE BAR

NINE FINE IRISHMEN

New York–New York, 3790 Las Vegas Blvd S ☎ 866 815 4365, ⓦ ninefineirishmen.com. Daily 11am–11pm. Cover $5 Wed & Thurs, $10 Fri & Sat. MAP P.32, POCKET MAP C3

A genuine Irish pub, shipped in pieces from Ireland, celebrating Irish beer, food and, in the evening, music and dance too. A small patio out on the Strip looks over "Brooklyn Bridge". During the weekday Happy Hour (Mon–Thurs 2–5pm), Guinness and other beers cost $5 per pint.

RED SQUARE BAR

Mandalay Bay, 3950 Las Vegas Blvd S ☎ 702 632 7201, ⓦ mandalaybay.com. Mon–Thurs & Sun 4–11pm, Fri 4.30pm–midnight, Sat 4pm–midnight. MAP P.32, POCKET MAP B7

Both a bar and a restaurant, *Red Square* is designed to evoke all things Russian – the decadence of the tsars, the graphic style of the Communist era and the icy chill of the steppes. Unless you have a real penchant for caviar, the food is a bit too expensive to be worth it, but the bar is great, with its solid-ice counter-top and frozen vodka vault.

Clubs and music venues

HAKKASAN

MGM Grand, 3799 Las Vegas Blvd S ☎ 702 891 3838, Ⓦ hakkasanlv.com. Wed–Sun 10.30pm–dawn. Cover men $20, women $10. MAP 32, POCKET MAP D3

Said to be the largest club in the world, an offshoot of what was originally a Chinese restaurant in London, this colossal, multi-level place incorporates two separate full-sized nightclubs, plus all sorts of dining rooms, ultra-lounges and private gardens; superstar DJs attract up to 7500 clubbers at weekends.

HOUSE OF BLUES

Mandalay Bay, 3950 Las Vegas Blvd S ☎ 702 632 7600, Ⓦ www.houseofblues.com. Daily 7am–midnight. MAP P.32, POCKET MAP B6

The national *House of Blues* music chain has recently revamped its Las Vegas outlet, in the heart of Mandalay Bay. While retaining its funky, voodoo-esque feel, the capacity has been reduced to a more intimate 1300. Individual concerts are interspersed with longer artist residencies; thus Carlos Santana has been signed up for regular long-term stints, with ticket prices from $89.

LAX

Luxor, 3900 Las Vegas Blvd S ☎ 702 262 5279, Ⓦ luxor.com. Thurs–Sat 10.30pm–4am. Cover men $30, women $20. MAP P.32, POCKET MAP B6

This offshoot of Hollywood's hot *LAX* nightclub can be a victim of its own success; the whole place, from the dramatic staircase to the long dance floor, gets way too crowded for comfort on big nights. If money is no object, skip the queues by paying for VIP table

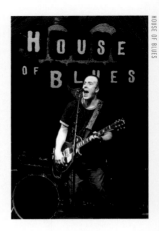

HOUSE OF BLUES

service. If you're happy with the mainstream music choices it's up there with Las Vegas's best.

LIGHT

Mandalay Bay, 3950 Las Vegas Blvd S ☎ 702 632 4700, Ⓦ thelightvegas.com. Wed, Fri & Sat 10.30pm–4am. Cover charge varies. MAP P.32, POCKET MAP B7

Mandalay Bay pulled off a real coup by hosting the first-ever Cirque du Soleil nightclub, designed to keep visitors to *Michael Jackson One* dancing all night. Holding over two thousand clubbers, it features a mobile DJ booth that rises from the floor, plus live Cirque performers. In summer, *Daylight* (Ⓦ daylightvegas.com), the beach club, stages outdoor pool parties and evening concerts.

Shows

BLUE MAN GROUP

Luxor, 3900 Las Vegas Blvd S ☎ 800 557 7428, Ⓦ blueman.com. Daily 7pm & 9.30pm; $86–188. MAP P.32, POCKET MAP B6

The hilariously postmodern Blue Men are Las Vegas favourites; kids love their craziness, adults their cleverness. Mute and lurid blue from head to toe, they combine paint-splashing, cereal-spewing clowning with pounding percussion and amazing visual effects.

CRISS ANGEL – MINDFREAK LIVE!

Luxor, 3900 Las Vegas Blvd S ☎702 262 4400, ⓦluxor.com. Wed–Sun 7pm & 9.30pm. $65–143. MAP P.32, POCKET MAP A6

Although *Mindfreak Live!* bears the Cirque brand, it's basically a showcase for everything Angel does best, blending close-up trickery with mind-blowing illusions to create a thrilling magic show. Beyond the pyrotechnics and heavy metal, he's essentially a hard-working, old-fashioned audience-pleaser.

KÀ

MGM Grand, 3799 Las Vegas Blvd S ☎702 531 3826, ⓦcirquedusoleil.com. Mon–Wed, Sat & Sun 7pm & 9.30pm. $75–196. MAP P.32, POCKET MAP D2

There's more martial-arts muscularity to this Cirque spectacular than to their other, more ethereal offerings; sceptics are guaranteed to find the set-piece stunts enacted on its tilting, rotating stage absolutely jaw-dropping. Add in extraordinary puppetry and sumptuous costumes, and while the twins-in-jeopardy storyline may leave you unmoved, *Kà* is certain to expand your horizons.

TOURNAMENT OF KINGS

Excalibur, 3850 Las Vegas Blvd S ☎702 597 7600, ⓦexcalibur.com. Mon & Fri 6pm, Wed, Thurs, Sat & Sun 6pm & 8.30pm. $66 including dinner. MAP P.32, POCKET MAP A4

This swashbuckling swords-and-slapstick supper show plunges family audiences into a jousting contest, complete with villainous black knights and maidens in peril. Ideal for anyone who'd rather eat chicken with their fingers than sit through Shakespeare.

ZUMANITY

New York–New York, 3790 Las Vegas Blvd S ☎702 740 6815, ⓦcirquedusoleil.com. Mon & Sun 9.30pm Tues, Fri & Sat 7pm & 9.30pm. $69–120, or $125 per person for a "duo sofa". All shows over-18s only. MAP P.32, POCKET MAP B3

While the concept – Cirque goes sexy – may pique your curiosity, the reality is disappointing, undercutting the erotic potential of fit bodies performing astonishing feats with pratfalls and smut. At times, it looks amazing, but it's no substitute for Cirque at their peak.

Wedding chapel

LITTLE CHURCH OF THE WEST

4617 Las Vegas Blvd S ☎702 739 7971, ⓦlittlechurchlv.com. Daily 8am–11pm. MAP P.32, POCKET MAP C9

This cute little chapel really is old, by Las Vegas standards; built for the Last Frontier casino in 1942, it has since migrated south to a spot half a mile beyond Mandalay Bay. With its tranquil garden, it feels a world away from the big-casino chapels. Packages range from the $199 "Let's Elope" to the $2975 "Unforgettable VIP Package".

LITTLE CHURCH OF THE WEST

CityCenter and around

When MGM Resorts opened the CityCenter complex, in 2009, the aim was to add a whole new neighbourhood to Las Vegas, giving the city a new kind of sleek, corporate architecture. By building a self-contained enclave set back from the Strip, they would vastly increase the value of what was previously unused land, and finally make it possible to expand east–west. A massive financial gamble, the project involved a huge new casino, Aria; a high-end shopping mall, Crystals; and several hotel-and-condo skyscrapers. A new neighbourhood has indeed appeared, stretching from the open-air Park in the south, adjoining the soon-to-be-renamed Monte Carlo, as far as the now-veteran Bellagio to the north. The one fly in the ointment is the brash new Cosmopolitan, cheekily added to the one tiny speck of Strip real estate that MGM didn't own.

MONTE CARLO/PARK MGM

3770 Las Vegas Blvd S ☎ 702 730 7777, Ⓦ montecarlo.com, Ⓦ parkmgm.com. MAP P.45, POCKET MAP C2

With the unveiling of CityCenter, the low-profile **Monte Carlo** casino became increasingly prominent in the plans of owners MGM. Ten years on, the space between the Monte Carlo and New York–New York has been transformed into a largely pedestrianized plaza known as **The Park**, and is home to the huge, multi-purpose **T-Mobile Arena** (see p.53). At the time of writing, the Monte Carlo remained open but was being overhauled, in preparation for being re-branded in 2018 as the **Park MGM**. Alongside the **Park Theater** concert venue (see p.53), the new complex is expected to hold an Italian marketplace, **Eataly**, with restaurants and food counters, and a nominally distinct 300-room boutique hotel, **NoMad**.

THE PARK

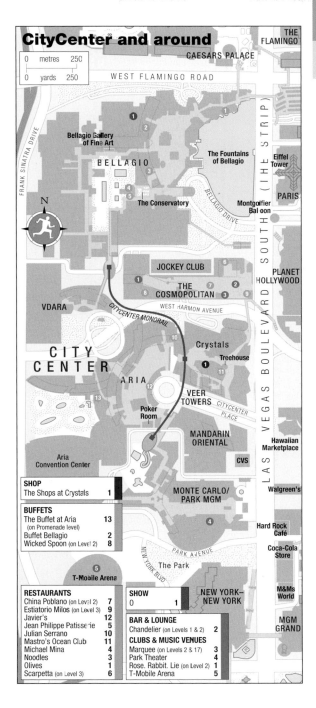

CityCenter and around

| 0 | metres | 250 |
| 0 | yards | 250 |

THE FLAMINGO

CAESARS PALACE

WEST FLAMINGO ROAD

Bellagio Gallery of Fine Art

BELLAGIO

The Fountains of Bellagio

Eiffel Tower

PARIS

The Conservatory

Montgolfier Balloon

N

SOUTH (THE STRIP)

BELLAGIO DRIVE

JOCKEY CLUB

PLANET HOLLYWOOD

THE COSMOPOLITAN

VDARA

CITYCENTER MONORAIL

WEST HARMON AVENUE

CITY CENTER

Crystals

Treehouse

ARIA

LAS VEGAS BOULEVARD

VEER TOWERS

CITYCENTER PLACE

Poker Room

MANDARIN ORIENTAL

Hawaiian Marketplace

CVS

Walgreen's

Aria Convention Center

MONTE CARLO/ PARK MGM

Hard Rock Café

Coca-Cola Store

PARK AVENUE

The Park

NEW YORK BLVD

T-Mobile Arena

M&Ms World

NEW YORK– NEW YORK

MGM GRAND

SHOP	
The Shops at Crystals	1

BUFFETS	
The Buffet at Aria (on Promenade level)	13
Buffet Bellagio	2
Wicked Spoon (on Level 2)	8

RESTAURANTS	
China Poblano (on Level 2)	7
Estiatorio Milos (on Level 3)	9
Javier's	12
Jean Philippe Patisserie	5
Julian Serrano	10
Mastro's Ocean Club	11
Michael Mina	4
Noodles	3
Olives	1
Scarpetta (on Level 3)	6

SHOW	
O	1

BAR & LOUNGE	
Chandelier (on Levels 1 & 2)	2
CLUBS & MUSIC VENUES	
Marquee (on Levels 2 & 17)	3
Park Theater	4
Rose. Rabbit. Lie (on Level 2)	1
T-Mobile Arena	5

45

CRYSTALS

CRYSTALS

3720 Las Vegas Blvd S ☎ 702 590 9299, Ⓦ theshopsatcrystals.com. MAP P.45, POCKET MAP B1 & F9

As the one public component of CityCenter to abut the Strip, **Crystals** certainly catches the eye. Designed by Daniel Libeskind, its jagged, colourful facade makes a contrast with the white walls and air-conditioned cool of its interior. Its primary role is as a (hugely expensive) shopping mall, **The Shops at Crystals** (see p.50).

Purely as a spectacle, however, Crystals is well worth a quick walk-through. At one point, it was planned as an urban park, and it features some extravagant, playful wooden structures, including the intricate 70ft **Treehouse**, home to the stylish *Mastro's Ocean Club* restaurant (see p.51), as well as a pair of arching wooden "pods".

There's also plenty of water on show, including the swirling glass-encased **fountains** on the lower floor, and some dazzling **sculptures** of neon light.

THE COSMOPOLITAN

3708 Las Vegas Blvd S ☎ 702 698 7000, Ⓦ www.cosmopolitanlasvegas.com. MAP P.45, POCKET MAP F9

At first glance, most Las Vegas visitors assume that **The Cosmopolitan**, facing Planet Hollywood (see p.54) across the Strip, is just one more piece of the modernist jigsaw puzzle that comprises CityCenter. It's not; it's an entirely separate luxury casino-hotel, stacked up vertically rather than sprawling horizontally, and impishly squeezed atop the former Jockey Club car park, slap in front of CityCenter, which MGM never managed to buy up.

Since opening in 2010, the Cosmopolitan has made itself very much at home in this prime spot, seducing locals and tourists alike with its glitzy architectural flourishes, high-profile **Marquee** nightclub (see p.53), excellent array of appealing restaurants just steps away from the Strip, and general evocation of glamorous days gone by. In the evenings especially, its buzzing public spaces tend to jostle with excited crowds.

The Cosmopolitan is a throwback to the old Las Vegas, when each casino was separately owned and run, acted like the rest of the city didn't exist, saw its business as being all about gambling and nightlife rather than shopping, and aimed to keep visitors on site by making it all but impossible to find the exits. Be warned that the Cosmopolitan also has the last laugh on CityCenter: while you might understandably assume that you could simply walk all the way through the building and reach Aria (see p.47), you can't – there's no pedestrian through route.

ARIA

3730 Las Vegas Blvd S ☎ 702 590 7111. 🌐 www.aria.com. MAP P.45, POCKET MAP B1

Although the CityCenter "neighbourhood" is supposed to be easy to explore on foot, you're only likely to visit **Aria**, the casino at its heart, if you make a very deliberate effort to reach it. Pedestrians can get here outdoors by following its hot, exposed approach road 250 yards west from the Strip, or more comfortably indoors, via the Crystals mall or the much longer walkways through Bellagio (see p.48) and the Monte Carlo (see p.44). A gleaming sci-fi **monorail** also connects Aria with both those properties, but the stations are so far back from the Strip that you gain very little by using it.

From the outside, with its sleek, curving skyscrapers, Aria looks more like a sophisticated big-city corporate HQ than a casino. The traffic circle in front of its main entrance holds a pulsating **fountain**, while to the left, more water cascades down a sleek, glistening black wall, 24ft tall.

Aria also identifies itself more with, say, Chicago than Las Vegas, by eschewing billboards, video screens and neon in favour of prestigious **contemporary art**. Sculptors represented include Henry Moore, one of whose signature abstractions stands in the tiny gap between Aria and Crystals; Claes Oldenburg, responsible for the giant typewriter eraser near the Strip; Antony Gormley, whose *Feeling Material* hangs from the ceiling; and Maya Lin, whose 84ft silver casting of the Colorado River stretches above the check-in desks.

While Aria's dazzling modernism certainly makes a welcome contrast with traditional Las Vegas aesthetics, in the end, of course, it's all in the service of Mammon – and more specifically, gambling. There's plenty more cutting-edge design to admire as you walk through the casino proper – don't miss the **Poker Room** fringed by gigantic golden playing cards – but there's little reason to linger unless your intention is to gamble.

Both the upper and lower levels of Aria hold a fine roster of restaurants, bars and cafés, but there are very few shops. Devoid of slots and gaming tables, the upper level can feel cavernously empty unless the **Convention Center** is in full swing.

When Aria opened it was home to a Cirque du Soleil tribute show to Elvis Presley. An unlikely fit for such a forward-looking property, the show swiftly ended its run, as did its replacement, Cirque's **Zarkana**. With the showroom now closed, Aria has shifted its focus to the Park Theater instead.

ARIA

BELLAGIO

3600 Las Vegas Blvd S ☎ 702 693 7111,
ⓦ bellagio.com. MAP P.45, POCKET MAP F7

Ranking high among Las Vegas's absolute must-see casinos, **Bellagio** proudly surveys the Strip across the graceful dancing fountains of its own broad, semicircular lake. This cream-coloured vision of Italian elegance was unveiled in 1998 as the final great flourish of the twentieth century's fastest-growing new city. It was the handiwork of legendary entrepreneur Steve Wynn, who spared no expense in his bid to follow his success with the Mirage (see p.68) by building the greatest hotel the world had ever seen. His original idea was to model it on a French Mediterranean beach and call it Beau Rivage; that changed after he visited the village of Bellagio, beside Lake Como in Italy.

Although Wynn himself is no longer at the helm – when MGM bought out his Mirage corporation in 2000, he took the money and ran down the street to start again – Bellagio is still going strong, racking up the highest turnover and biggest profits in the city. It's also larger than ever, having thrust a tentacle southwards to create an indoor walkway down to CityCenter. As Bellagio's northeast corner is just a few steps across a pedestrian bridge from Caesars Palace (see p.58), many sightseers use it as a corridor to stay out of the sun as they head south, creating a constant flow of visitors.

Almost all of Bellagio's Strip facade is taken up with waterfront restaurants, so once you're inside you won't see much of the lake. Similarly, its colonnaded pool area is only open to guests. Even so, the sheer opulence of the main casino floor is astounding, and several of the public areas should not be missed. In addition to the **Conservatory**, be sure to walk through the hotel lobby, where a vast chandelier of multicoloured glass flowers, created by sculptor Dale Chihuly, swarms across the ceiling. And take a glance behind the check-in counter to see the Roman gardens, accessible to employees only.

When Bellagio first opened, the management briefly attempted to impose a dress code and bar the children of non-guests. Las Vegas's democratic open-to-all traditions soon put paid to that policy, however, so there's

BELLAGIO

nothing snooty about the crowds you'll see window shopping in the exclusive stores of the small Via Bellagio shopping arcade, or gasping at the menu prices for its magnificent but undeniably expensive restaurants. Other than the building itself, the two most popular attractions that bring in visitors from elsewhere are the **buffet** (see p.50) and Cirque du Soleil's long-running, breathtaking water spectacular, **O** (see p.53).

THE CONSERVATORY

THE FOUNTAINS OF BELLAGIO

Bellagio, 3600 Las Vegas Blvd S. Mon–Fri 3–8pm every 30min, 8pm–midnight every 15min; Sat noon–8pm every 30min, 8pm–midnight every 15min; Sun 11am–3pm every 15min, 3–8pm every 30min, 8pm–midnight every 15min. Free. MAP P.46, POCKET MAP F7

Even when it's lying dormant, Bellagio's ice-blue eight-acre lake makes an impressive spectacle in the Nevada desert. When it erupts into a balletic extravaganza of jetting **fountains**, as it does from morning/early afternoon until midnight daily, it's the best free show in town. The sky-high spurts and streams are accompanied by booming music – mostly songs from Broadway shows and popular classics. For anyone other than diners in the expensive waterfront restaurants the best views are either from the Strip sidewalk (stake your place early), from the top of the Eiffel Tower in Paris (see p.57) or from the guest rooms in either Paris (see p.118) or the Cosmopolitan (see p.115).

THE CONSERVATORY

Bellagio, 3600 Las Vegas Blvd S. Open 24hr. Free. MAP P.46, POCKET MAP E8

Ever since Bellagio opened, its magnificent **Conservatory** has been considered one of the major sights of the city. A glassed-over courtyard ringed by galleries and restaurants, it's repeatedly transformed by a huge team of gardeners into extravagant themed shows that include bizarre whimsical props amid an extraordinary array of living plants. The five separate seasonal displays start with the Chinese New Year and then celebrate spring, summer, autumn and winter. During the week it takes to dismantle each show and prepare the next, there's nothing to see.

BELLAGIO GALLERY OF FINE ART

Bellagio, 3600 Las Vegas Blvd S ☎ 702 693 7871, ⓦ bellagio.com. Daily 10am–8pm. $17. MAP P.46, POCKET MAP E7

Originally home to Steve Wynn's own art collection, the **Bellagio Gallery of Fine Art** managed to survive Wynn's departure and continues to put on changing exhibitions that generally last for around six months. The entrance fee is high for such a small space though, and only worth paying for the better shows, such as the 2012–13 display of twenty paintings by Claude Monet, which was curated in conjunction with the Museum of Fine Arts in Boston.

THE SHOPS AT CRYSTALS

Shop

THE SHOPS AT CRYSTALS

3720 Las Vegas Blvd S ☎ 702 590 5299,
Ⓦ theshopsatcrystals.com. Mon–Thurs &
Sun 10am–11pm, Fri & Sat 10am–midnight.
MAP P.45, POCKET MAP F9

Pitched at Las Vegas's proverbial
"whales"– high-rolling big
spenders – the glitzy Shops at
Crystals makes no bones about
being very high-end indeed.
With its sparkling white walls,
and exquisite sculptural
features, few dare stray into
boutiques belonging to
designers such as Paul Smith
and Stella McCartney.

Buffets

THE BUFFET AT ARIA

Promenade Level, Aria, 3730 Las Vegas Blvd S
☎ 702 590 7111, Ⓦ aria.com. Breakfast Mon–Fri
7–11am $22; lunch Mon–Fri 11am–3.30pm $26;
brunch Sat & Sun 7am–3.30pm $32; dinner
daily 3.30–10pm, Mon–Thurs $37, Fri–Sun $42.
MAP P.45, POCKET MAP A2

Choices at CityCenter's one
buffet are more limited than
elsewhere, but the food is a cut
above. The sushi and Indian
specialities are excellent and the
desserts are the best in town.

Pay $13 extra for unlimited
beer, wine, champagne or
Bloody Marys. An entire lobster
is served at your table during
weekend dinners.

BUFFET BELLAGIO

Bellagio, 3600 Las Vegas Blvd S ☎ 702 791
7111, Ⓦ bellagio.com. Breakfast Mon–Fri
7–11am $22; lunch Mon–Fri 11am–3.30pm
$26; brunch Sat & Sun 7am–3.30pm $33 (or
$45 with champagne); dinner daily 3.30–10pm,
Mon–Thurs $37, Fri & Sat $42.
MAP P.45, POCKET MAP E7

The first "gourmet buffet" in
town sparked standards, and
less happily prices, to rise all
over Las Vegas. While no longer
quite as exceptional, it still
features an amazing array of
food; even for breakfast you can
have salmon smoked or baked
and omelettes cooked to order,
with fillings such as crabmeat.

WICKED SPOON

Level 2, The Cosmopolitan, 3708 Las Vegas
Blvd S ☎ 702 698 7000, Ⓦ www.cosmopolitan
lasvegas.com. Brunch Mon–Thurs 8am–2pm
$28, Fri–Sun 8am–3pm $36; dinner Mon–
Thurs 5–9pm $42; Fri & Sat 3–10pm $49;
Sun 3–9pm $49. MAP P.45, POCKET MAP J6

Although the Cosmopolitan's
buffet is hard to find, right at the
back upstairs, plenty of visitors
make their way here to enjoy a
wide range of carefully prepared
cuisines. Most are served as
individual portions, though you
can take as many as you like.
There's no breakfast; fill up with
a late-morning brunch instead.

Restaurants

CHINA POBLANO

Level 2, The Cosmopolitan, 3708 Las Vegas
Blvd S ☎ 702 698 7900, Ⓦ chinapoblano.com.
Mon–Thurs & Sun 11.30am–11pm, Fri & Sat
11.30am–11.30pm. MAP P.45, POCKET MAP K6

The concept of combining Asia
and Mexico goes back a long
way – *china poblana* is the

national dress of Mexico. Here, in what looks like a street café, it is Chinese and Mexican cuisines that are blended. Only a few dishes, like the $18 Huitlacoche noodles, literally mix the two, but by picking and choosing you can make yourself an interesting, good-value meal.

ESTIATORIO MILOS

Level 3, The Cosmopolitan, 3703 Las Vegas Blvd S ☏ 702 698 7930, ⓦ milos.ca. Mon–Thurs 5.30–11.30pm, Fri 5.30pm–midnight, Sat noon–2.30pm & 5.30pm–midnight, Sun noon–2.30pm & 5.30–11pm. MAP P.45, POCKET MAP K7

Vast urns and exquisite statues adorn this beautiful Greek restaurant. For lunch there's a fantastic $25 set menu; in the evening your choice from the array of fresh fish, flown in daily from Athens, will arrive at your table cooked to perfection, and costs around $50 per person.

JAVIER'S

Casino Level, Aria, 3730 Las Vegas Blvd S ☏ 866 590 3637, ⓦ aria.com. Daily 11.30am–midnight. MAP P.45, POCKET MAP B1

Spectacular Mexican restaurant, complete with terrifying wooden carvings, that serves all the standard dishes, scrupulously prepared, for around $20 – a build-your-own-tacos plate for two costs $50 – as well as inventive variations like lobster enchiladas for $30, and shrimp, steak and seafood mains at up to $50.

JEAN PHILIPPE PATISSERIE

Bellagio, 3600 Las Vegas Blvd S ⓦ jpchocolates .com. Mon–Thurs 6am–11pm, Fri–Sun 6am–midnight. No reservations. MAP P.45, POCKET MAP E8

It takes rare self-discipline to walk past Jean-Philippe Maury's extraordinary bakery without pausing to swoon at its central feature; the world's largest chocolate fountain swirls around the entire room, cascading

through endless funnels and pipettes. The urge to stop for a $5 mug of hot chocolate, if not a pastry, is all but overwhelming.

JULIAN SERRANO

Casino Level, Aria, 3730 Las Vegas Blvd S ☏ 877 230 2742, ⓦ aria.com. Mon–Thurs 11.30am–11pm, Fri 11.30am–11.30pm, Sat 10.30am–11.30pm, Sun 10.30am–11pm. MAP P.45, POCKET MAP F9

One of Las Vegas's biggest hits of recent years, this beautiful tapas bar tastes even better than it looks. Most tapas cost $12–15 for a small portion; be sure to branch out and sample fabulous creations like the cocoa butter balls filled with chilled gazpacho. Larger mains include paella for two from $45.

MASTRO'S OCEAN CLUB

Crystals, 3720 Las Vegas Blvd S ☏ 702 798 7115, ⓦ www.mastrosrestaurants.com. Daily 5–11pm. MAP P.45, POCKET MAP B1

Even the new Las Vegas still has a penchant for a good old-fashioned steakhouse, though this one stands out from the crowd not so much for its heavy-duty $50-plus rib-eyes as its amazing setting; reserve early and you get to dine in the bowers of Crystals' whimsical wooden Treehouse.

JEAN PHILIPPE PATISSERIE

MICHAEL MINA

Bellagio, 3600 Las Vegas Blvd S ☎ 702 693 7223, ⓦ www.michaelmina.net. Mon–Sat 5.30–10pm. MAP P.45, POCKET MAP E8

In his flagship restaurant adjoining Bellagio's Conservatory, Egyptian-born Michael Mina continues to reinvent his tried and tested classics. Starters like tuna tartare with mint cost up to $28, while mains range from $42 to the $55 filo-dusted Dover sole and Mina's signature lobster pot pie. The chef's tasting menu costs $128 (wine pairings $88 extra); there's a no-choice vegetarian menu for $85; and at 5.30pm or 6pm you can enjoy a $68 pre-theatre menu.

NOODLES

Bellagio, 3600 Las Vegas Blvd S ☎ 702 693 8131, ⓦ bellagio.com. Daily 11am–2am. MAP P.45, POCKET MAP F8

Bellagio's casual, walk-ins only, pan-Asian diner, off the main casino floor behind the *Baccarat* bar, is well worth seeking out. Its intriguing decor looks great and the food, with cuisines ranging from Thai and Vietnamese, to Chinese and Japanese, is no disappointment. Noodle dishes are around $18 and at weekend lunchtimes dim sum typically costs around $9.

OLIVES

Bellagio, 3600 Las Vegas Blvd S ☎ 702 693 8865, ⓦ bellagio.com. Daily 11.30am–10.30pm. MAP P.45, POCKET MAP F7

This elegant modern American restaurant offers an experience to savour. For a light meal, opt for an $18 flatbread topped perhaps with fig and prosciutto. Full mains tend to be pricier, with pasta dishes at over $40 and steaks over $50, but the succulent roasted chicken costs $22 at lunch, $29 for dinner.

SCARPETTA

Level 3, The Cosmopolitan, 3708 Las Vegas Blvd S ☎ 702 698 7960, ⓦ www.cosmopolitanlasvegas.com. Daily 6–11pm. MAP P.45, POCKET MAP K7

Courtesy of "new Italian" chef Scott Conant, the food is even better than the view at *Scarpetta*, which has huge panoramic windows overlooking the Bellagio fountains. All of Las Vegas has flocked to enjoy starters like his $18 tuna "susci", and mains including short rib and bone marrow agnolotti (stuffed pasta; $25). For the full works, go for the $110 set menu.

Bars and lounges

CHANDELIER

Cosmopolitan, 3708 Las Vegas Blvd S ☎ 702 698 7979, ⓦ www.cosmopolitanlasvegas.com. Casino level open 24hr, other levels hours vary. MAP P.45, POCKET MAP K6 & F9

Beneath the dazzling, dangling canopy of the eponymous two-million-crystal chandelier, the Cosmopolitan's centrepiece bar soars through three separate levels. It's the middle floor where the action is, with DJ music and a buzzy crowd.

SCARPETTA

CHANDELIER

Clubs and music venues

MARQUEE

Levels 2 and 17, The Cosmopolitan, 3708 Las Vegas Blvd S ☎ 702 333 9000, Ⓦ marqueelasvegas.com. Nightclub Mon & Thurs–Sat 10pm–4am; Dayclub daily 10am–7pm in summer. Cover varies $25–100. MAP P.45, POCKET MAP F9 & K6

This cutting-edge indoor-outdoor nightclub with a pool-centred "dayclub", features a 50ft-high main floor, the Boombox, overlooking the Strip, and the Library, which has pool tables. The dayclub is smaller than at Encore (see p.82), but attracts bigger-name DJs and celebs. Add in drinks and the dollars add up; buy a wristband for the whole weekend.

PARK THEATER

Monte Carlo, 3770 Las Vegas Blvd S ☎ 844 600 7275, Ⓦ www.montecarlo.com. See website for schedule. MAP P.45, POCKET MAP B2

Five-thousand-seat indoor arena, with a larger stage than the Colosseum at Caesars Palace, that's primarily used for live music. So far it's hosted residencies by the likes of Cher,

Ricky Martin and Bruno Mars, with prices ranging $55–205.

ROSE.RABBIT.LIE

Level 2, The Cosmopolitan, 3708 Las Vegas Blvd S ☎ 877 667 0585, Ⓦ cosmopolitan lasvegas.com. Wed–Sat 6pm–midnight; cover for special events. MAP P.45, POCKET MAP 16

Self-proclaimed "modern supper club", targeted at The Cosmopolitan's hipster clientele, that remains deliberately hard to categorize. Having abandoned the avant-garde performance-art show with which it opened, it now stages retro-style gigs, and one-off events, and serves excellent cocktails and bar food.

T-MOBILE ARENA

3780 Las Vegas Blvd S ☎ 702 692 1300, Ⓦ www.t-mobilearena.com. See website for schedule. MAP P.45, POCKET MAP A3

Set back from the Strip between New York–New York and the Monte Carlo (now known as The Park), this huge covered stadium was unveiled in 2016 as the centrepiece of The Park development. Holding twenty thousand spectators, and home to the Vegas Golden Knights hockey team, it has put on gigs by Kanye West, Barbra Streisand and the Rolling Stones, plus boxing matches, basketball games and award ceremonies. Concert tickets range $55–250.

Shows

O

Bellagio, 3600 Las Vegas Blvd S ☎ 702 693 8866, Ⓦ cirquedusoleil.com. Wed–Sun 7pm & 9.30pm. $138–217. MAP P.45, POCKET MAP E7

This phenomenal show centres on a metal-mesh stage, any part of which can suddenly disappear beneath the performers' feet. The dazzling array of death-defying leaps and plunges create a show you'll never forget.

The Central Strip

Long the scene of fierce inter-casino rivalries, the central portion of the Strip now feels much more like a pedestrian neighbourhood, where visitors stroll from one casino to the next thanks to new outdoor spaces like the Linq development adjoining the Flamingo and the Roman Plaza outside Caesars Palace. What's not obvious, however, is that all those casinos, from the block-spanning Caesars Palace to grizzled veterans like the Flamingo and Harrah's across the Strip, and newcomers like Paris and Planet Hollywood to the south, now belong to the same conglomerate; you'd never guess that it was Harrah's that came out on top.

PLANET HOLLYWOOD

3667 Las Vegas Blvd S ☎ 866 919 7472,
🌐 planethollywoodresort.com. MAP P.55,
POCKET MAP G9

The only Strip giant saddled with a brand name not otherwise known for gambling, **Planet Hollywood** has struggled to establish a strong identity; it's not part of the dining chain or even an independent entity. The building itself opened in 2000 as a new version of the long-established Aladdin, where Elvis Presley married Priscilla in 1966. Planet Hollywood took it over in 2004, after the Aladdin went broke in the wake of 9/11, but

they in turn soon floundered and sold out to Harrah's in 2010.

Planet Hollywood has subsequently raised its profile by signing Britney Spears for a long-term residency. As the Aladdin, though, it always seemed to be empty, thanks to the design flaw that meant the door from the Strip was too hard to find – simply rectified by erecting a huge sign reading "Casino Entrance". The main attraction within is the **Miracle Mile** mall (see p.56); the actual casino is relatively small, and is largely targeted, with its blaring music and flashing lights, at "hip" young visitors.

PLANET HOLLYWOOD

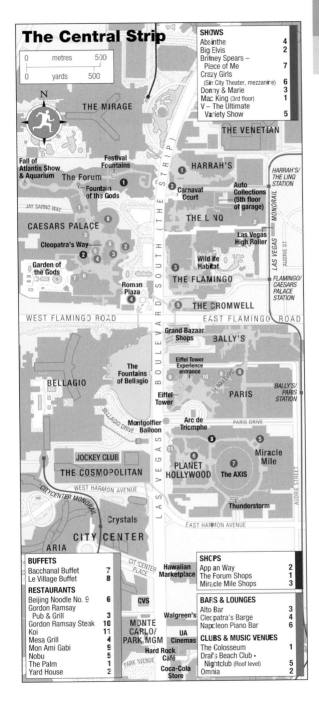

The Central Strip

| 0 | metres | 500 |
| 0 | yards | 500 |

N

THE MIRAGE

THE VENETIAN

SHOWS

Absinthe	4
Big Elvis	2
Britney Spears – Piece of Me	7
Crazy Girls (Sin City Theater, mezzanine)	6
Donny & Marie	3
Mac King (3rd floor)	1
V – The Ultimate Variety Show	5

Fall of Atlantis Show & Aquarium

The Forum

Festival Fountains

HARRAH'S

Carnaval Court

Auto Collections (5th floor of garage)

HARRAH'S/ THE LINQ STATION

Fountain of the Gods

JAY SARNO WAY

CAESARS PALACE

THE LINQ

Cleopatra's Way

Las Vegas High Roller

Garden of the Gods

Wild life Habitat

THE FLAMINGO

FLAMINGO/ CAESARS PALACE STATION

LAS VEGAS AUDRIE ST

MONORAIL

Roman Plaza

THE CROMWELL

WEST FLAMINGO ROAD

EAST FLAMINGO ROAD

Grand Bazaar Shops

BALLY'S

The Fountains of Bellagio

Eiffel Tower Experience entrance

BELLAGIO

PARIS

BALLY'S/ PARIS STATION

Eiffel Tower

BELLAGIO DRIVE

Montgolfier Balloon

Arc de Triomphe

PARIS DRIVE

JOCKEY CLUB

THE COSMOPOLITAN

WEST HARMON AVENUE

PLANET HOLLYWOOD

The AXIS

Miracle Mile

AUDRIE STREET

CITYCENTER MONORAIL

Crystals

CITY CENTER

Thunderstorm

EAST HARMON AVENUE

ARIA

CITYCENTER PLACE

BUFFETS

| Bacchanal Buffet | 7 |
| Le Village Buffet | 8 |

RESTAURANTS

Beijing Noodle No. 9	6
Gordon Ramsay Pub & Grill	3
Gordon Ramsay Steak	10
Koi	11
Mesa Grill	4
Mon Ami Gabi	9
Nobu	5
The Palm	1
Yard House	2

Hawaiian Marketplace

CVS

Walgreen's

MONTE CARLO/ PARK MGM

PARK AVENUE

Hard Rock Café

Coca-Cola Store

UA Cinemas

SHOPS

App an Way	2
The Forum Shops	1
Miracle Mile Shops	3

BARS & LOUNGES

Alto Bar	3
Cleopatra's Barge	4
Napoleon Piano Bar	6

CLUBS & MUSIC VENUES

The Colosseum	1
Drai's Beach Club • Nightclub (Roof level)	5
Omnia	2

MIRACLE MILE

Planet Hollywood, 3663 Las Vegas Blvd S
☎ 702 866 0704, ⓦ www.miraclemileshopslv
.com. MAP P.55, POCKET MAP G8

Coiled like an enormous snake around and through Planet Hollywood, the **Miracle Mile** mall is nonetheless an entirely separate operation. Built at the same time as the new Aladdin, in 2000, and still bearing traces of its original Arabian Nights theming, it was credited by some as being responsible for the Aladdin's financial failure; given the chance to stroll into a mall without having to walk through a casino en route, Strip sightseers simply ignored the Aladdin altogether. Besides a free **"thunderstorm" attraction**, the Miracle Mile holds a wide range of bars, restaurants and theatres to complement the clothing boutiques, shoe shops and galleries (see p.62).

PARIS

3655 Las Vegas Blvd S ☎ 877 796 2096,
ⓦ parislasvegas.com. MAP P.55, POCKET MAP G8

Designed by the architects previously responsible for New York–New York, and opened a few months before the millennium, **Paris** represented the final flourish of the Las Vegas craze for building entire miniature cities. Its exterior remains one of the Strip's most enjoyable spectacles, surmounted by a gigantic Eiffel Tower whose legs crash through the ceiling into the heart of the casino itself, and anchored by the Arc de Triomphe, the Opera and a Montgolfier hot-air balloon, which becomes a glowing landmark at night.

Although it's slightly misleading to think of Paris as a separate casino at all – it was originally built as an extension to Bally's (see p.57) next door, to which it's linked by a broad corridor at the back of the building – it was an immediate hit. With both of these properties now owned by Caesars Entertainment, the tail these days is clearly wagging the dog, and Bally's feels like a minor adjunct to Paris.

Pleasing Parisian touches, such as the ironwork that echoes the city's Metro stations, still abound throughout the interior. From the excellent **buffet** to the pastry shops and bridal-wear boutiques, the great majority of Paris's shops, restaurants and bars have some sort of French connection.

PARIS

Much of it is tongue-in-cheek, so even the more tenuous links, as in calling the sports bar the **Bar du Sports**, are just part of the fun. The one area where visitors have balked at the Gallic flavour has been entertainment; Paris has long since abandoned its hopes of staging all-French productions (like, say, *Phantom of the Opera* or *Les Miserables*) in favour of safer options like Barry Manilow and Engelbert Humperdinck.

BALLY'S

EIFFEL TOWER EXPERIENCE

Paris, 3655 Las Vegas Blvd S ☎ 888 727 4758, ⓦ www.caesars.com/paris-las-vegas. Mon–Fri 9.30am–12.30am, Sat & Sun 9.30am–1am. $14 daytime, $19 evening. MAP P.55, POCKET MAP E8

Towering 540ft over the Strip, Las Vegas's version of the **Eiffel Tower** is half the height of the Seine-side original. It's not simply a half-sized replica, however; if it was, you wouldn't be able to squeeze into the elevators, for example. In addition, this one is made of steel not iron, and doesn't have a public staircase to the top.

Visitors can either dine in the luxury restaurant 100ft up, or buy a ticket inside Paris's main entrance for the **Eiffel Tower Experience** and ride all the way to the summit viewing platform. While it offers great views all day long, the prime time to come is in the evening; as its builders always cheekily intended, the Eiffel Tower makes the perfect vantage point for watching the Bellagio fountains.

BALLY'S

3645 Las Vegas Blvd S ☎ 877 603 4390, ⓦ www.caesars.com/ballys-las-vegas. MAP P.55, POCKET MAP G7

These days, you could easily fail to notice **Bally's**, set well back from the Strip opposite Bellagio. When it opened in 1973, however, this was the MGM Grand, the biggest hotel in the world. Only after a terrible hotel fire killed 84 people here in 1980 was it bought and renamed by the gaming manufacturer Bally's, and a new MGM Grand constructed further south. Now owned by Caesars Entertainment, Bally's has become a humdrum casino that was mainly noteworthy for hosting the throwback revue show *Jubilee!*.

Bally's was built in the era when casinos still needed huge Strip-front car parks. Legendary in Las Vegas lore as the landing site for Nicolas Cage and the parachuting Elvises in the 1992 movie *Honeymoon in Vegas*, and subsequently spanned by a network of neon-covered walkways, the former Bally's car park has now at last been built over to become the site of an open-air mall, the **Grand Bazaar Shops**. The small booths and kiosks are largely devoted to snacks and souvenirs, so it's hardly a must-see attraction, but it's one more step towards making the Strip truly pedestrian-friendly.

CAESARS PALACE

3570 Las Vegas Blvd S ☎ 866 227 5938, 🌐 caesarspalace.com. MAP P.55, POCKET MAP F6

Still a Las Vegas headliner in its own right, fifty years since it was built, **Caesars Palace** remains arguably the biggest name on the Strip. During the casino-building spree either side of the millennium, it slipped for a moment behind its newer rivals, to the point where Harrah's Entertainment were able to buy up control. Recognizing the prestige value of the name, however, they've not only reinvigorated Caesars and put it back on top, but changed their own name to Caesars Entertainment.

Caesars Palace was originally the creation of **Jay Sarno**, a hard-gambling associate of legendary Teamsters leader Jimmy Hoffa. Cobbled together for just $24 million, it was unveiled in 1966, complete with clerks dressed as Roman centurions and cocktail waitresses kitted out like Cleopatra. Sarno himself doubled his money and sold out in 1969; he moved on to build Circus Circus, and eventually died of a heart attack in a suite at Caesars in 1984.

As well as coming up with the Caesars Palace name, designed to appeal to American and European gamblers alike, Sarno also decreed that the one thing it will never have is an apostrophe – it does not belong to Caesar, it's filled by the thousands of Caesars who choose to visit it. His crucial legacy, however, was that he'd set Caesars up on an expanse of land – originally rented from Kirk Kerkorian, who remained a major Las Vegas player until his death in 2015 – that has so far proved big enough to hold every enlargement architects have been able to imagine.

STATUE, CAESARS PALACE

Pausing to admire Caesars Palace from the Strip is one of the great joys of visiting Las Vegas. White marble Classical statues are everywhere you look, from Julius Caesar forever hailing a cab on the main driveway to the Winged Victory of Samothrace guarding a row of gently cascading pools. Most impressive of all are the ornate fountains that surround the entrance to the Forum mall.

The central bulk of Caesars Palace is still proudly set back around 150 yards from the Strip; all that space between the casino and the Strip originally held an enormous car park. Once Las Vegas visitors began to arrive by plane instead of by car, the gap became a deterrent to pedestrians. It was Caesars that pioneered the use of long moving walkways to haul them in – and naturally neglected to build corresponding outbound walkways to let them back out again. Bit by bit, the space has been built over. First, at the northern end, the vast **Forum** mall (see p.59) steadily extended until it reached all the way to the Strip; then the mighty **Colosseum** appeared alongside, in 2003; and more recently the **Roman Plaza** has burgeoned at the south, and now holds bars, restaurants and even, currently, a circus marquee, which is home to the *Absinthe* show (see p.66).

Inside, Caesars Palace bewilders most first-time visitors. Unlike newer Las Vegas properties, designed to be user-friendly and let you find what you're looking for, Caesars was laid out in the hope that gamblers might never be able to escape.

Making your way between the casino itself and the Forum is easy enough; the two simply meet on the casino floor. However, exploring the rest of Caesars Palace is less straightforward. A network of narrow and circuitous corridors lead to the older **Appian Way** mall, which offers the chance of a close-up inspection, from directly below, of Michaelangelo's naked *David*, and Cleopatra's Way, home to the Egyptian-themed *Cleopatra's Barge* nightclub (see p.65).

Much of the rest of the property, including the luxurious **Garden of the Gods** pool complex, based on the baths of Pompeii, is only open to registered guests.

THE FORUM

3500 Las Vegas Blvd S ☎ 702 893 3807, ⓦ www.simon.com/mall. MAP P.55, POCKET MAP F5

By opening the **Forum** mall in 1992, Caesars Palace not only became the first Strip casino to turn both shopping and dining into major reasons to visit Las Vegas, it also created one of the city's most iconic attractions.

Though widely copied ever since, the Forum's domed false-sky ceiling still packs a mind-blowing punch. Designed to evoke the skyline of ancient Rome, it cycles hourly between the dazzling blue of "day" and the orange glow of "night".

Sadly, though, many of the kitschier elements of the Forum's earlier years, such as the animatronic "living statues" that adorned its centrepiece fountains, have been discarded in favour of ever more opulent and ornate decor. The most striking feature these days is the amazing convoluted spiral escalator at the Forum's main Strip entrance. Its separate moving pathways follow different trajectories, so you can never be sure they'll take you where you want to go.

The **Forum Shops** themselves still rank as Las Vegas's premier shopping spot (see p.62).

THE FORUM

THE CROMWELL

3595 Las Vegas Blvd S ☎ 702 777 3777, ⓦ www.caesars.com/cromwell. MAP P.55, POCKET MAP G7

Squeezed into a sandwich-sized slot at one of Las Vegas's prime intersections, the Strip's smallest casino used to be a budget alternative, known originally as the Barbary Coast and since 2007 as Bill's Gamblin' Hall & Saloon. It reopened in 2014, however, as a self-styled "boutique hotel", **The Cromwell**.

For no obvious reason, the name is intended to evoke Parisian splendour rather than those titans of English history, Thomas and Oliver. Its 188 rooms are now luxurious and expensive, while the principal new features are **Giada**, an Italian restaurant run by TV chef Giada de Laurentiis, and **Drai's** (see p.66), a massive indoor-outdoor rooftop club; the entire structure had to be strengthened to support the colossal weight of its various pools and pavilions.

THE FLAMINGO

3555 Las Vegas Blvd S ☎ 702 733 3111, ⓦ www.caesars.com/flamingo-las-vegas. MAP P.55, POCKET MAP G6

Now that it's just another glossy casino, shoulder to shoulder in the Strip's endless procession of identikit giants, it's all but impossible to picture **the Flamingo** in its original form. Whatever anyone may tell you, when it opened in 1946 it wasn't the very first Strip resort of them all. Standing alone in the desert, however, a mile south of its nearest neighbour, the Last Frontier, the Flamingo was an enticing hundred-room oasis that put Las Vegas on the map as a glamorous, even dangerous, getaway.

Not that the Flamingo was an immediate hit. So disastrously over-budget that it was forced to close within a fortnight, its initial failure cost owner Benjamin "Bugsy" Siegel his life, when his fellow mobsters gunned him down the next year. By then, however, the Flamingo was already going strong, and a wave of imitators was starting to appear.

With Bugsy a distant, sanitized memory, the Flamingo these days is much more Donny and Marie – long-term residents in its showroom – than Don Corleone. Its current owners, Caesars Entertainment, target it largely at older visitors who remember Las Vegas as it used to be back in the 1980s, when the Flamingo was still the biggest hotel in the world, and before everything had to keep reinventing itself to suit the latest trend.

From its superb neon sign and the Strip-facing patio of *Jimmy Buffet's Margaritaville* at the front, to the real-life flamingoes and penguins in the free **Wildlife Habitat** and

THE FLAMINGO

garden-set pool complex around the back, there's a lot to like about the Flamingo. As the Linq development next door expands, further upgrades and improvements will doubtless follow.

THE LINQ

3535 Las Vegas Blvd S ☎ 800 634 6441, Ⓦ thelinq.com. MAP P.55, POCKET MAP G5
Caesars Entertainment responded to MGM Resorts' construction of CityCenter by carving out its own rival "neighbourhood". Centring on the showpiece **High Roller**, it took what was previously a narrow roadway between the Flamingo and Imperial Palace casinos, and turned it into a broader pedestrian corridor of shops, bars and restaurants.

The long-standing Imperial Palace was not demolished, but totally "re-skinned", with its previous Japanese facade stripped away and its interior decor transformed. Briefly re-christened the Quad, it has now appropriated the name of the entire project – **the Linq**.

New features include a 32-lane bowling alley with its own restaurant, plus a tattoo studio, a "sneaker boutique" opened by rapper Nas, and several bars.

For the moment, one final relic of the Imperial Palace survives – the **Auto Collections**, a remarkable array of vintage cars, most of them for sale, on the fifth floor of the garage – but that will surely vanish soon.

LAS VEGAS HIGH ROLLER

3545 Las Vegas Blvd S ☎ 702 322 0593, Ⓦ thelinq.com. Daily 11.30am–2am. $26 11.30am–7pm, $37 7pm–2am. MAP P.55, POCKET MAP H6
The world's largest observation wheel, the **Las Vegas High Roller**, stands just off the Strip at the far end of the pedestrianized Linq entertainment district. At 550ft tall, it's over a hundred feet taller than the similar, 443ft London Eye, and rotates non-stop. Each of its 28 see-through cabins can carry up to forty passengers. The long-range panoramas are spectacular, though intervening buildings mean it doesn't offer ground-level views of the Strip.

HARRAH'S

3475 Las Vegas Blvd S ☎ 800 214 9110, Ⓦ www.caesars.com/harrahs-las-vegas. MAP P.55, POCKET MAP G5
Harrah's is the great unsung success story of the Strip. When all its rivals were going crazy for adding eye-catching, child-friendly gimmicks, constructing replica cities and enticing young hipsters to day-night pool parties, Harrah's just carried on giving their parents the same old, same old formula of cheap eats, plentiful slots and middle-of-the-road entertainment. And it did it all so well that one by one Harrah's swallowed up all of its Central Strip rivals. Then, having bought the lot, the Harrah's organization simply changed its name to Caesars Entertainment; it's as if it never happened.

For anyone under a certain age, Harrah's itself remains as boring as ever. Walk past on the Strip, and your attention may be captured by the performers on the open-air **Carnaval Court** stage, but step inside and you're in a soporific time warp, where country superstar Toby Keith's *I Love This Bar & Grill!* is the biggest attraction. To be fair, Harrah's does put on some good-value daytime shows, including Mac King (see p.67) and *Big Elvis* (see p.66), but it's no place for thrill-seeking sightseers.

THE FORUM SHOPS

Shops

APPIAN WAY

Caesars Palace, 3570 Las Vegas Blvd S ☎ 702 731 7222, ⓦ www.caesars.com/caesars-palace. Store hours vary. MAP P.55, POCKET MAP F6

Much smaller than the Forum, the **Appian Way** is arrayed along two corridors just off the casino floor at Caesars Palace. Centring on an 18ft marble replica of Michaelangelo's *David*, it includes upscale jewellery stores, high-end crafts at Martin & MacArthur, and a shop selling Caesars' merchandise.

THE FORUM SHOPS

3500 Las Vegas Blvd S ☎ 702 893 3807, ⓦ www.simon.com/mall. Mon–Thurs & Sun 10am–11pm, Fri & Sat 10am–midnight. MAP P.55, POCKET MAP F5

Still going strong after a quarter of a century, the Forum Shops is foot-for-foot the country's most successful mall. That's partly because its big-name brands tend to be squeezed into smaller spaces than usual. While its two main "streets" are hardly full of surprises – expect to see an Apple Store, Gap and H&M, for example – they do offer a very intense burst of shopping.

MIRACLE MILE SHOPS

Planet Hollywood, 3663 Las Vegas Blvd S ☎ 888 800 8284, ⓦ www.miraclemileshopslv .com. Mon–Thurs & Sun 10am–11pm, Fri & Sat 10am–midnight. MAP P.55, POCKET MAP G8

Give or take the odd fountain, the largest casino mall, the Miracle Mile Shops, could be just about anywhere. Easily entered straight from the Strip, it really is a mile long; walk from one end to the other and you'll pass a huge range of stores, from mall staples like Urban Outfitters, American Apparel, French Connection and Quiksilver to some jaw-droppingly awful "art galleries" and a couple of ABC convenience stores.

Buffets

BACCHANAL BUFFET

Caesars Palace, 3570 Las Vegas Blvd S ☎ 702 731 7928, ⓦ www.caesars.com /caesars-palace. Brunch Mon–Fri 7.30am–3pm $40, champagne brunch Sat & Sun 8am–3pm $50; dinner Mon–Fri 3–10pm $55, Sat & Sun 3–10pm $58. MAP P.55, POCKET MAP F6

The Strip's latest gourmet buffet – much the best at any Caesars-owned property – opened in 2012. It features five hundred freshly made items daily, from sushi, dim sum and pho soup to fresh oysters and wood-fired pizzas, prepared by chefs at nine separate "show kitchens".

LE VILLAGE BUFFET

Paris, 3655 Las Vegas Blvd S ☎ 702 946 7000, ⓦ www.parislasvegas.com. Breakfast Mon–Fri 7–11am $22, Sat & Sun 7–10am $24; lunch Mon–Fri 11am–3pm $25; champagne brunch Sat & Sun 10am–3pm $31; dinner Mon–Thurs & Sun 3–10pm, $31, Fri & Sat 3–10pm, $34. MAP P.55, POCKET MAP G7

Unique in focusing on a single cuisine – or rather, on French cuisine, from Brittany to Provence – *Le Village* offers the

The Buffet of Buffets

Buffet fans should watch out for the **Buffet of Buffets pass**, sold at all the buffets in every Caesars-owned casino, which allows 24-hour unrestricted access to them all for a total cost of $60 on weekdays, $75 at weekends. Use it to eat at, say, 8pm one night, 7pm the next, and you get two dinners into the bargain. Note, however, that each visit to the *Bacchanal Buffet* at Caesars Palace or the *Carnival World Buffet* at the Rio costs extra.

most satisfying meal of any casino buffet. You'll find a wider array elsewhere, but if you're partial to French meat or fish, or simply fancy a fresh baguette and all the cheese you can eat, in a playful themed setting, don't miss it.

Restaurants

BEIJING NOODLE NO. 9

Caesars Palace, 3570 Las Vegas Blvd S
☎ 877 346 4642, ⓦ www.caesars.com
/caesars-palace. Daily 11am–10.30pm.
MAP P.55, POCKET MAP F6

Approached via aquariums that hold a thousand goldfish and resembling a pale, mysterious, underwater cavern, this Chinese noodle shop is one of Las Vegas's most enjoyable places to eat. Fortunately, the food matches the setting, though with dim

sum buns and dumplings at around $13, and the (large) noodle dishes more like $20, so too do the prices.

GORDON RAMSAY PUB & GRILL

Caesars Palace, 3570 Las Vegas Blvd S
☎ 702 731 7410, ⓦ caesars.com/caesars
-palace. Mon–Thurs & Sun 11am–11pm, Fri &
Sat 11am–midnight. MAP P.55, POCKET MAP F6

Stylized version of a British pub, run by TV chef and new Las Vegas darling Gordon Ramsay, with some tables adjoining the casino floor and the rest inside, close to a bar decked out with pretend red phone kiosks. Fish and chips cost $30, steak-and-ale pies $25, while the many draught beers cost $9 during the "Hell's Kitchen" Happy Hour, weekdays 2–5pm.

GORDON RAMSAY STEAK

Paris, 3655 Las Vegas Blvd S ☎ 877 346
4642, ⓦ www.caesars.com/paris-las-vegas.
Daily 4.30–10.30pm. MAP P.55, POCKET MAP G7

For his first Las Vegas venture, perfectionist pottymouth Gordon Ramsay played it safe, opening a high-class steakhouse near Paris's main entrance – its tunnel approach represents the trip from France to England, incidentally. Diners select from a trolley laden with marbled, aged slabs of prime meat; a superbly cooked veal chop costs $50, a strip steak $63 and the $145 tasting menu includes Beef Wellington.

BEIJING NOODLE NO. 9

MON AMI GABI

KOI

Planet Hollywood, 3667 Las Vegas Blvd S
☎ 702 454 4555, ⓦ koirestaurant.com.
Mon–Thurs & Sun 5.30–10.30pm, Fri & Sat
5.30–11.30pm. MAP P.55, POCKET MAP G8

While not the celebrity favourite
it is in Hollywood, this fancy
restaurant serves tasty Japanese
food at what, for Las Vegas, are
reasonable prices – especially
considering its views of Bellagio's
fountains. Sushi rolls, tuna
tartare or tempura shrimp cost
well under $20, mains like
steamed sea bass or wasabi short
ribs up to $30.

MESA GRILL

Caesars Palace, 3570 Las Vegas Blvd S ☎ 877
346 4642, ⓦ mesagrill.com. Mon–Fri 11am–
2.30pm & 5–11pm, Sat & Sun 10.30am–3pm &
5–11pm. MAP P.55, POCKET MAP F6

Contemporary Southwestern
chef Bobby Flay, who made his
name in New York, has shown
enough commitment to his Las
Vegas outlet, across from the
Colosseum entrance, for it to
become Caesars' most
dependable fine-dining spot.
Mexican-influenced favourites
include sixteen-spice chicken,
which costs $18 in a lunch
salad, more like $33 for dinner.

MON AMI GABI

Paris, 3655 Las Vegas Blvd S ☎ 702 944
4224, ⓦ www.monamigabi.com. Mon–Thurs
& Sun 7am–11pm, Fri & Sat 7am–midnight.
MAP P.55, POCKET MAP G7

Among the first Las Vegas
restaurants to offer al fresco
dining, this exuberant
evocation of a Paris pavement
brasserie remains the city's
premier lunchtime pick. For
a real taste of France, you can't
beat a $15 *croque-madame*
(ham, cheese and egg
sandwich) for breakfast; *moules
frites* (mussels and chips) for
lunch ($14 or $26); or *steak
frites* for dinner ($29).

NOBU

Caesars Palace, 3570 Las Vegas Blvd S
☎ 702 785 6628, ⓦ noburestaurants.com.
Mon–Thurs & Sun 5–11pm, Fri & Sat 5pm–
midnight. MAP P.55, POCKET MAP F6

Flagship restaurant for the
world-spanning empire of
Japanese-Peruvian chef Nobu
Matsuhisa, whose fans are so
devoted that Caesars even has
its own Nobu hotel tower into
the bargain. Ambience and
audience alike are very
upmarket; and the food is
exquisite, with hot mains
including black cod miso for
$37 or beef tenderloin for $36,
and full chef's-choice tasting
menus starting at $125.

THE PALM

Forum Shops, Caesars Palace ☎ 702 732
7256, ⓦ thepalm.com. Daily 11.30am–11pm.
MAP P.55, POCKET MAP F5

A veteran of the Forum scene,
this offshoot of the legendary
New York steakhouse offers
a stylish, surprisingly formal
escape from the shopping
mania outside. For lunch, $16
will buy you a salad, burger
or sandwich. In the evening,
classic Italian veal dishes cost
$34–36, and a prime, 24oz
rib-eye steak is $55.

YARD HOUSE

Linq Promenade, 3545 Las Vegas Blvd S
☎ 702 597 0434, ⓦ yardhouse.com. Mon–Thurs
& Sun 11am–1am, Fri & Sat 11am–1.30am. MAP
P.55, POCKET MAP H5

Lively restaurant/bar along the
pedestrian mall that leads to
the High Roller, where the
extensive food menu ranges
from jambalaya or Southern
fried chicken to a vegetarian
quinoa salad, all priced at well
under $20. They also offer craft
ales and ciders from around
the world, many of which you
can indeed drink from a
genuine "yard".

Bars and lounges

ALTO BAR

Caesars Palace, 3570 Las Vegas Blvd S
☎ 702 731 7778, ⓦ caesars.com/caesars
-palace. Mon, Wed & Thurs 9am–2am,
Tues 9am–4am, Fri–Sun 24hr. MAP P.55,
POCKET MAP F6

Catch your breath after walking
Caesars' endless hallways in
this up-to-the-minute
open-fronted lounge, which
replaced the much-missed
Seahorse Lounge in 2016.
Raised above the casino floor,
and specializing in very fancy
cocktails at $16–21 – a beer
costs $8 – it's the perfect spot
to see and be seen, though
you can also hide away in a
private booth.

CLEOPATRA'S BARGE

Caesars Palace, 3570 Las Vegas Blvd S
☎ 702 731 7333, ⓦ caesars.com/caesars
-palace. Tues–Thurs 7pm–2am, Fri & Sat
7pm–3am. MAP P.55, POCKET MAP F6

Caesars Palace was built just
three years after Elizabeth
Taylor's iconic performance as
Cleopatra; centred on a floating
replica of a Pharaonic barge,

surrounded by gilded furniture
and campy little nooks, this
bar's been here ever since. A
glorious reminder of Las
Vegas's golden era, it never
charges for admission, though
every night sees appearances by
either live musicians or DJs.

NAPOLEON PIANO BAR

Paris, 3655 Las Vegas Blvd S ☎ 702 946
7000, ⓦ caesars.com/paris-las-vegas.
Daily 4pm–1am. No cover charge. MAP P.55,
POCKET MAP F5

Come in the early evening to
this plush, dimly lit, bordello-
red bar, poised halfway along
the internal corridor that
connects Paris to Bally's and,
while there may be a lounge
act on stage, like a vocal
group or comedian, it still feels
like a sophisticated venue at
which to enjoy a glass of
champagne, cognac, cocktails
or cigars. Between 9pm and
1am nightly, however, things
turn much more raucous, as
duelling pianists vie to belt out
whatever tunes the audience
requests (and is prepared to
tip for) – expect there to be
energetic, enthusiastic
sing-along renditions of
Bohemian Rhapsody and
the like.

YARD HOUSE

Clubs and music venues

THE COLOSSEUM

Caesars Palace, 3570 Las Vegas Blvd S ☎ 866 227 5938, ⓦ thecolosseum.com. Showtimes and prices vary; Celine Dion typically ranges from $55–250. MAP P.55, POCKET MAP F5

Built in 2003 to house a long-term residency by Celine Dion, the 4000-seat Colosseum is the last great stronghold of the old-style Las Vegas headliner. Celine still returns frequently, while Elton John, Rod Stewart and Mariah Carey also play regular extended engagements. Stars who appear for a night or two have included Jerry Seinfeld and Van Morrison.

DRAI'S BEACHCLUB • NIGHTCLUB

The Cromwell, 3595 Las Vegas Blvd S ☎ 702 777 3800, ⓦ draislv.com. Nightclub Thurs–Sun 10.30pm–4am; Beach Club summer only daily 11am–6pm. Cover $20. MAP P.55, POCKET MAP G7

This huge indoor-outdoor night/ day club, on The Cromwell's roof, enjoys the best Strip views. Named for EDM entrepreneur and film producer Victor Drai, previously responsible for creating XS at Encore and Tryst at Wynn Las Vegas, it has big-name DJs and live performers – Kendrick Lamar for New Year 2016–17– plus go-go dancers, with poolside cabanas for high-rollers.

OMNIA

Caesars Palace, 3570 Las Vegas Blvd S ☎ 702 785 6200, ⓦ omnianightclub.com. Tues & Thurs–Sun 10.30pm–4am. Cover $20–50. MAP P.55, POCKET MAP F6

Unveiled in 2015 as the successor to the massively popular Pure, this club boasts a huge open-air Strip-view terrace. Ordinary mortals can expect a long queue, and astonishing

ABSINTHE

prices for drinks ($28 for a beer) for what is truly a once-in-a-lifetime Las Vegas experience, with the world's biggest DJs.

Shows

ABSINTHE

Caesars Palace, 3570 Las Vegas Blvd S ☎ 800 745 3000, ⓦ absinthevegas.com. Wed–Sun 8pm & 10pm. $109–134. MAP P.55, POCKET MAP F6

Staged in the round, in a marquee on Caesars' outdoor Roman Plaza, this no-holds-barred circus-tinged burlesque show has taken Las Vegas by storm. Conceived as a crude and abrasive counterpoint to the fey whimsy of Cirque du Soleil, and eschewing PC in all its forms, it's more of a drunken night out than a traditional show, but it still charges Cirque-level prices.

BIG ELVIS

Piano Bar, Harrah's, 3475 Las Vegas Blvd S ☎ 702 369 5111, ⓦ www.caesars.com /harrahs-las-vegas. Mon, Wed & Fri 2–6pm. Free. MAP P.55, POCKET MAP G5

Las Vegas's biggest and best-loved Elvis impersonator, Pete Vallee, has shucked off the pounds in the last few years to become merely Large Elvis.

His King-like voice still packs a powerful punch, though, and his mastery of Elvis's repertoire and easy audience rapport – requests welcome – make this the best free show in town.

BRITNEY SPEARS – PIECE OF ME

Planet Hollywood, 3667 Las Vegas Blvd S 702 777 2782, caesars.com/planet -hollywood. Schedule varies seasonally; usually Wed, Fri & Sat 9pm, $55–210. MAP P.55, POCKET MAP H9

The girl from Kentwood, Louisiana has reinvented herself as Las Vegas's consummate post-millennial headliner. Britney lip-synchs – but there is a live band – as she flings herself around the stage in a stunning show. All kinds of premium packages are available, culminating in the opportunity to "meet and greet" Britney.

CRAZY GIRLS

Planet Hollywood, 3667 Las Vegas Blvd S 702 777 2782, caesars.com/p.aret -hollywood. Daily 9pm, $54–98 No under-21s. MAP P.55, POCKET MAP G8

Newly relocated from the sadly missed Riviera casino, the Strip's best-known "adult revue" remains a throwback to the Vegas of yesteryear. Half a dozen topless, if not exactly crazy, sequin-encrusted showgirls dance through a medley of show tunes, and there's an interlude of comedy and magic.

DONNY & MARIE

The Flamingo, 3555 Las Vegas Blvd S 702 777 2782, caesars.com/flamingo -las-vegas. Tues–Sat 7.30pm, $104–250. MAP P.55, POCKET MAP G6

Anyone who doesn't need to ask the surname of this brother-and-sister duo will know what to expect – family-friendly service with a smile. As well as singing their combined hits, each does his or her own thing, and there's lots of new material, which in

Donny's case includes a "hip-hop" routine. The old-style showroom seating is at shared tables, with drink service.

MAC KING

Harrah's, 3475 Las Vegas Blvd S 702 693 6143, mackingshow.com. Tues–Sat 1pm & 3pm. $38 & $49. MAP P.55, POCKET MAP G5

Just so there's no doubt, Mac King is billed as a comedy magician. With his clownish country-boy persona, clean-talking patter, easy way with his audience and family-friendly prices – plus of course his stunning sleight of hand – he's Las Vegas's best daytime entertainment bargain.

V – THE ULTIMATE VARIETY SHOW

Miracle Mile, Planet Hollywood, 3663 Las Vegas Blvd S 866 932 1818, vtheshow .com. Mon–Thurs & Sun 8.30pm, Fri & Sat 7pm & 8.30pm. $70 or $90. MAP P.55, POCKET MAP H8

This enjoyable, long-running variety show features established acts and crowd-pleasing routines. Regulars include "hip-hop contortionist" Turf; gloriously deadpan Mexican juggler Wally Eastwood; and Russ Merlin, whose Halloween mask audience-volunteer stunt brings the house down.

DONNY & MARIE

The North Strip

Along the North Strip a vibrant cluster of high-end properties compete to grab visitors' attention with gimmicks like volcanoes (the Mirage), Renaissance bridges (the Venetian) and all-round gilded opulence (Wynn Las Vegas). This part of the Strip is where things turn personal, with the giant casinos owned by fiercely competitive tycoons: specifically, Sheldon Adelson, owner of the Venetian and the Palazzo, is locked in fierce rivalry with Steve Wynn, of the similarly twinned Wynn Las Vegas and Encore. Until recently, the North Strip was regarded as stretching almost all the way to downtown. Since the recession kicked in, however, almost all the veteran casinos that lay further north have either closed down or been blown up, while most of the projects scheduled to replace them have been abandoned.

THE MIRAGE

3400 Las Vegas Blvd S ☎ 702 791 7111, ⓦ mirage.com. MAP P.70, POCKET MAP F4

Unveiled as entrepreneur Steve Wynn's first Strip venture, in 1989 – when Las Vegas seemed to be in decline, and no new Strip hotels had been built for sixteen years – the **Mirage** can justly claim to have changed the city overnight. Proving that by investing in luxury, glamour and spectacle, casinos could bring back the crowds, it spawned such a host of imitators that now, ironically, it no longer stands out from the pack. Following endless mergers and buy outs, it now belongs to MGM Resorts, which tends to concentrate its attention on its string of properties further south, while the long-departed Wynn himself has built his latest opulent resort, Wynn Las Vegas (see p.72), a short way north.

There's still plenty to like about the Mirage, from its

glassed-in atrium, complete with towering tropical trees, via its well-judged array of restaurants and bars, to its huge complex of pools and gardens, part of which is home to the **Secret Garden and Dolphin Habitat**. It's also still at the top of the entertainment tree, having replaced uber-camp German magicians Siegfried and Roy with the Beatles showcase, *Love* (see p.84) and amazing impressionist Terry Fator (see p.85).

Steve Wynn's most radical innovation was to target the Mirage at pedestrians wandering the Strip in search of things to do. Hence the artificial **volcano** outside, which erupts at hourly intervals, on the hour, after dark.

VOLCANO, THE MIRAGE

SECRET GARDEN AND DOLPHIN HABITAT

Mirage, 3400 Las Vegas Blvd S ☏ 702 791 7188, ⓦ miragehabitat.com. Daily 10am–7pm. Adults $22, ages 4–12 $17. MAP P.70, POCKET MAP E4

Although a wayward tiger sadly curtailed the performing careers of Siegfried and Roy in 2003, the menagerie of big cats that featured in their magic is still here. Cages in the **Secret Garden and Dolphin Habitat** contain everything from black leopards and golden tigers to their signature white lions and tigers. There are also two pools of bottlenose dolphins, which interact with visitors.

TI (TREASURE ISLAND)

3300 Las Vegas Blvd S ☏ 702 894 7111, ⓦ treasureisland.com. MAP P.70, POCKET MAP G3

TI (Treasure Island) was built in 1993 as a sort of kid brother to the Mirage (see p.68) next door, with an all-pervasive pirate theme aimed at family visitors. While it's still physically connected to the Mirage by a free **monorail**, it's now under separate ownership, and distances itself from its yo-ho-ho past by using the anodyne acronym TI.

The most prominent feature of Treasure Island during its first twenty years was the shallow **lagoon** in front, home to twin replica pirate ships that were crewed first by battling buccaneers and then later by gyrating, bikini-clad "sirens" whose after-dark music-and-dance shows lured in vast crowds. Architectural theorists tied themselves in knots arguing whether Treasure Island was a building, a performance space or a theme park. Ships and sirens alike have now gone, prosaically replaced by a crass Mexican "party restaurant", *Senor Frog's*, and a huge CVS grocery/pharmacy.

Phil Ruffin, former owner of the now-vanished New Frontier, bought TI in 2008, when MGM Resorts ran short of cash to build CityCenter. He's steadily turning it into a blue-collar joint, home to nightspots like *Gilley's Saloon* (see p.81), though he's hung on to Cirque's first-ever Las Vegas show, *Mystère* (see p.84).

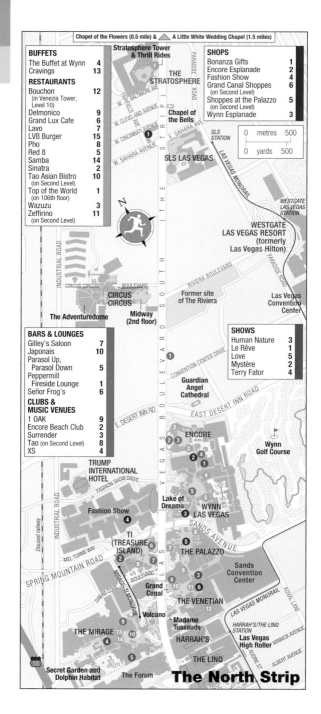

Chapel of the Flowers (0.5 mile) & A Little White Wedding Chapel (1.5 miles)

BUFFETS

The Buffet at Wynn	4
Cravings	13

RESTAURANTS

Bouchon (in Venezia Tower, Level 10)	12
Delmonico	9
Grand Lux Cafe	6
Lavo	7
LVB Burger	15
Pho	8
Red 8	5
Samba	14
Sinatra	2
Tao Asian Bistro (on Second Level)	10
Top of the World (on 106th floor)	1
Wazuzu	3
Zeffirino (on Second Level)	11

SHOPS

Bonanza Gifts	1
Encore Esplanade	2
Fashion Show	4
Grand Canal Shoppes (on Second Level)	6
Shoppes at the Palazzo (on Second Level)	5
Wynn Esplanade	3

BARS & LOUNGES

Gilley's Saloon	7
Japonais	10
Parasol Up, Parasol Down	5
Peppermill Fireside Lounge	1
Señor Frog's	6

CLUBS & MUSIC VENUES

1 OAK	9
Encore Beach Club	2
Surrender	3
Tao (on Second Level)	8
XS	4

SHOWS

Human Nature	3
Le Rêve	1
Love	5
Mystère	2
Terry Fator	4

0 metres 500
0 yards 500

Stratosphere Tower & Thrill Rides

THE STRATOSPHERE

Chapel of the Bells

SLS Las Vegas

SLS STATION

LAS VEGAS MONORAIL

WESTGATE LAS VEGAS STATION

WESTGATE LAS VEGAS RESORT (formerly Las Vegas Hilton)

PARADISE ROAD

W. BALTIMORE AVE
W. CLEVELAND AVENUE
W. CINCINNATI AVENUE
E. SAHARA AVE
W. SAHARA AVENUE

THE STRIP (LAS VEGAS BOULEVARD SOUTH)

INDUSTRIAL ROAD

Riviera Boulevard

CIRCUS CIRCUS BOULEVARD

CIRCUS CIRCUS

The Adventuredome

Midway (2nd floor)

Former site of The Riviera

Las Vegas Convention Center

CONVENTION CENTER DRIVE

Guardian Angel Cathedral

E. DESERT INN RD

EAST DESERT INN ROAD

ENCORE

Wynn Golf Course

TRUMP INTERNATIONAL HOTEL

FASHION SHOW DRIVE

Fashion Show

Lake of Dreams

WYNN LAS VEGAS

SANDS AVENUE

THE PALAZZO

Sands Convention Center

TI (TREASURE ISLAND)

MEL TORME WAY

Disused railway

INDUSTRIAL ROAD

SPRING MOUNTAIN ROAD

MIRAGE MONORAIL

SIREN'S COVE BOULEVARD

Grand Canal

Volcano

THE VENETIAN

Madame Tussauds

LAS VEGAS MONORAIL

KOVAL LANE

HARRAH'S/THE LINQ STATION

Las Vegas High Roller

WINNICK AVENUE

THE MIRAGE

HARRAH'S

THE LINQ

AUDRIE ST

ALBERT AVENUE

Secret Garden and Dolphin Habitat

The Forum

The North Strip

THE VENETIAN

3355 Las Vegas Blvd S ☎ 702 414 1000, ⓦ www.venetian.com. MAP P.70 POCKET MAP G4

The hugely successful **Venetian** casino opened in 1999 on the site of the much-mourned Sands, the former Las Vegas home of Frank Sinatra and the Rat Pack. Even if its owner, Sheldon Adelson, may lack the design flair of Steve Wynn, he has an unarguable genius for making money. After buying the Sands in 1988, he amassed a billion-dollar fortune from the annual tech-industry trade show COMDEX and has more recently expanded his casino operations into Macau, as well as ploughing huge sums into conservative politics at home.

The Venetian itself is a re-creation of the ultimate honeymoon photo album; Adelson returned from his 1991 honeymoon trip to Venice with the idea of building a vast replica of the city. Around a dozen distinct Venetian landmarks squeeze side by side into the casino's Strip facade, while its main entrance lies between two columns, modelled on a pair brought to Venice's Piazza San Marco from Constantinople in 1172. One is topped by St Theodore, the city's original patron, the other by a winged lion representing St Mark, who became its patron in 1204.

The interior of the Venetian holds fewer specific echoes of the city. While it's the **Grand Canal** upstairs that draws in the sightseers, it's the sheer opulence elsewhere, from the huge staircases and resplendent frescoes to the endless hallways of marble tiles, which makes this the most impressive public space on the Strip. It's also among the busiest, thanks to an excellent crop of restaurants, shops and theatres, and the

Sands Convention Center at the back.

When it first opened, the Venetian out-trumped Bellagio's Gallery of Fine Art (see p.49) by opening two separate Guggenheim art museums. Both have long since disappeared, but the exhibition space near the hotel lobby is still used for occasional temporary art shows.

THE GRAND CANAL

Venetian, 3355 Las Vegas Blvd S ☎ 702 414 4300, ⓦ www.venetian.com. Gondola rides indoors Mon–Thurs & Sun 10am–11pm, Fri & Sat 10am–midnight; outdoors daily 11am–10pm. $29, $16 for a two-person private ride. MAP P.70, POCKET MAP G4 & K5

You can't have Venice without the **Grand Canal**. The Venetian has it twice – outdoors beside the Strip and as the centrepiece of its shopping and dining mall upstairs. While neither section is particularly large, let alone authentic, you have to admire the sheer nerve. With its artificial sky, the indoor segment is obviously modelled on the Forum and holds a large plaza based on St Mark's Square. Singing gondoliers take paying customers on short gondola rides along the canal.

THE GRAND CANAL

MADAME TUSSAUDS

Venetian, 3377 Las Vegas Blvd S ☎ 866 841 3739, Ⓦ www.madametussauds.com. Mon–Thurs & Sun 10am–9pm, Fri & Sat 10am–10pm. $30, ages 7–12 $20; twenty percent discount online. MAP P.70, POCKET MAP G4

Entered directly from the Strip, just off the Venetian's attractive covered Rialto Bridge, **Madame Tussauds** taps into Las Vegas's craving for close celebrity contact by allowing visitors to get personal with waxworks ranging from Brad Pitt and Daniel Craig to the bizarre body-painted Blue Men (even though they're not actually recognizable as individuals). With the single exception of the President in the White House, for whom there's an extra fee, you're free to take unlimited photos of, and with, all of your friendly, new-found waxy playmates.

THE PALAZZO

3325 Las Vegas Blvd S ☎ 702 607 7777, Ⓦ www.palazzo.com. MAP P.70, POCKET MAP H3

Even if owner Sheldon Adelson insists that his **Palazzo** resort is entirely separate from the Venetian next door, no one takes the distinction seriously; broad internal walkways enable visitors to step from one property to the other and barely notice the transition. Counted as a single unit, this would be, with over seven thousand rooms, the largest hotel in the world.

Considered on its own, on the other hand, the Palazzo is among the least interesting casinos in Las Vegas. As well as its own very high-end shopping mall and a decent crop of restaurants, it's home to the *Lavo* nightclub, but has nothing of any interest for casual sightseers. Even the giant butterflies added to jazz up its central waterfall feature look more like one of rival Steve Wynn's cast-off ideas than anything truly original.

WYNN LAS VEGAS

3131 Las Vegas Blvd S ☎ 702 770 7000, Ⓦ wynnlasvegas.com. MAP P.70, POCKET MAP J2

Steve Wynn, the man who's credited with inventing the new Las Vegas by opening first the Mirage and then Bellagio, bounced back from losing control of the Mirage organization by building his own self-named resort, **Wynn Las Vegas**, in 2005. Like his great rival at the Venetian-Palazzo next door, Sheldon Adelson, Wynn swiftly complemented Wynn Las Vegas with Encore, and now runs two nominally distinct resorts on the same site.

When Wynn bought this prime slice of real estate it held the fabled *Desert Inn*, where Howard Hughes lived out his final years in paranoid seclusion. Steve Wynn doesn't do secondhand, though; he blew the whole place up and set to work building bigger and better than ever. The result, a majestic bronze crescent soaring skywards alongside the similar Encore, is breathtaking. Rendered almost blind by a degenerative eye disease, Wynn loves to fill his casinos with vibrant, dazzling swathes of colour – hence the plush red carpets that sweep through the interior, leading to a flower-packed **central garden** where the trees are bedecked with fairy lights and lanterns.

Because Steve Wynn wanted every Las Vegas visitor to come and admire Bellagio and the Mirage, he gave them all sorts of crowd-pleasing novelties. Wynn Las Vegas, being targeted more exclusively at the luxury end of the market with its array of consistently high-end restaurants and nightspots, holds fewer specific attractions and is therefore not quite so much of a must-see. Its most unusual feature is the **Lake of Dreams**, an expanse of water illuminated at night with changing projections, and peopled by mysterious mannequins. Unlike the Mirage's volcano, it was deliberately designed to only be visible to visitors from inside the property.

ENCORE

3121 Las Vegas Blvd S ☎ 702 770 7000, Ⓦ wynnlasvegas.com. MAP P.70, POCKET MAP J1

Encore stands in the same relation to Wynn Las Vegas as does the Palazzo to the Venetian. Erected three years after its elder brother, in 2008, and joined to it seamlessly via plush corridors, it's every bit as lavish – this is where Prince Harry was photographed naked in 2012 – but offers little sense of identity in its own right. In a deliberate piece of provocative one-upmanship, Steve Wynn built it 11ft taller than rival Sheldon Adelson's Palazzo, unveiled earlier the same year. Adelson, it's widely believed, responded by opening a large, downmarket Walgreens pharmacy at the Palazzo's Strip-level corner, thumbing his nose at the pretentious shops preferred by Wynn.

Like all Wynn's properties, Encore is ablaze with colour, like an episode of *Sesame Street* that's brought to you by the colour Red and the insects Butterfly and Dragonfly. Other than the general air of luxury, its main strategy to bring in visitors is via entertainment.

The indoor-outdoor, day-night **Encore Beach Club** (see p.82) has been a huge hit, not least with visiting British royalty, while Steve Wynn pulled off a genuine coup by luring country superstar Garth Brooks out of retirement for a long-term deal. Brooks has now moved on, but Wynn has plenty more up his sleeve, including turning the golf course out the back into a giant tropical oasis.

ENCORE

GUARDIAN ANGEL CATHEDRAL

GUARDIAN ANGEL CATHEDRAL

302 Cathedral Way ☎ 702 735 5241,
🌐 dioceseoflasvegas.org. Masses Mon–Fri
8am & 12.10pm, Sat 4pm & 5.30pm, Sun 8am,
9.30am, 11am, 12.30pm & 5pm. MAP P.70,
POCKET MAP K1

Of all the Strip's eye-catching
architectural wonders, perhaps
the most unexpected stands
just north of Encore – the
Roman Catholic **Guardian
Angel Cathedral**. It was built
in 1963, on land donated by
the former owner of both the
Desert Inn and Stardust
casinos, Moe Dalitz, a Jewish
gangster from Detroit. Seeking
to improve his public image,
he paid modernist architect
Paul Revere Williams to
design this sloping tent-like
structure. A stained-glass
window to the right of the
altar serves as a memorial to
the Strip as it looked in the
1960s, depicting long-gone
casinos like the Sands, the
Stardust and the International.

CIRCUS CIRCUS

2880 Las Vegas Blvd S ☎ 702 734 0410,
🌐 circuscircus.com. MAP P.70, POCKET MAP K8

Guarded by the giant figure of
Lucky the Clown – if you
suffer from coulrophobia, or
fear of clowns, you won't like

Lucky one bit – the candy-
striped big top of **Circus
Circus** has loomed beside the
Strip for half a century. In
recent years, however, and
despite being owned by MGM
Resorts, Circus Circus has
been battered and isolated
by the recession. Former
neighbours including the New
Frontier and the Stardust have
disappeared, while few of the
fancy new developments that
were supposed to replace them
ever materialized – the
Fontainebleau Las Vegas was
constructed but never opened,
while ambitious plans to
build first Echelon (2008–
2014), and subsequently the
Asian-themed Resorts World
(2014–2016), which was
purportedly going to feature
live pandas, came to nothing.
Pedestrian traffic hereabouts
has dwindled to nothing, to
leave Circus Circus cut off
from the Strip in general, and
from MGM Resorts' other
properties in particular.

Circus Circus has always
been a strange, unsettling
hybrid of circus and casino.
It famously attracted the scorn
of Hunter S. Thompson, who
wrote in *Fear and Loathing in
Las Vegas* that "Circus Circus
is what the whole hep world
would be doing on Saturday
night if the Nazis had won the
war". When it opened, in 1968,
as Jay Sarno's attempt to repeat
his success with Caesars
Palace, it didn't include any
hotel rooms and charged
customers an entry fee. At first
it was very much an adult
playground, reflecting the
sleazier side of carnival
attractions. It took a few years
to hit on the formula it still
follows, of catering largely to
families by offering **live circus
acts** and other child-oriented
attractions. Coupled with its

low room rates, the result has been that Circus Circus has become the tackiest of the major Strip casinos.

Circus Circus is so huge that it's the only Strip casino to have an internal **monorail system**, to take guests to their rooms. With its low ceilings and endless corridors, lined with fast-food outlets and novelty stores, it's quite a maze, and it can be hard to find the mezzanine area that's home to the **Midway**. The circular stage here plays host to a constant succession of free circus acts, from trapeze artists and jugglers to tightrope walkers and, yes, clowns. Old-fashioned sideshows offer kids the chance to kick-start a lifetime's gambling habit by winning stuffed toys.

THE ADVENTUREDOME

Circus Circus, 2880 Las Vegas Blvd S ☎ 702 794 3939, ⓦ adventuredome.com. Daily 10am–midnight during school holidays, otherwise Mon–Thurs 11am–6pm, Fri & Sat 10am–midnight, Sun 10am–9pm. $6–12 individual attractions, $32 all-day wristband, children under 4ft $18. MAP P.70, POCKET MAP J8

Las Vegas's largest theme park, the **Adventuredome**, is housed

in a giant pink enclosure at the back of Circus Circus, a long walk from the Strip. Entirely indoors and on a much smaller scale than, say, Disney World or Universal Studios, it's aimed very much at children. Adults may well enjoy the twisting, looping **Canyon Blaster** and the even more ferocious, ultra-steep **El Loco**, but most of the space is given over to SpongeBob Squarepants simulator rides and the like.

SLS LAS VEGAS

2535 Las Vegas Blvd S ☎ 702 761 7757, ⓦ slslasvegas.com. MAP P.70, POCKET MAP L2

The veteran Sahara, a Strip fixture since 1952, fell victim to the recession and closed its doors in 2011. It was not actually demolished, though, simply stripped of its former *Arabian Nights* minarets and comedy camels, and given a glossy new facade plus an injection of Philippe Starck stylings, to reopen in 2014 as **SLS Las Vegas**.

Calling itself a "boutique resort" despite having three hotel towers and over 1600 rooms, SLS is part of a rapidly expanding nightlife and hotel chain with outlets in Beverley Hills, South Beach and New York. An entertainment-based property pitched a rung or two below the Strip's top tier, it's home to an indoor-outdoor pool and nightclub, *Foxtail*, plus big-name restaurants including *Bazaar Meat* and the Starck-designed sushi place *Katsuya*.

The vast empty lot across the Strip from SLS belongs to MGM Resorts. Despite sustaining huge losses when they staged the US version of the Rock in Rio festival here in 2015, they hope to use the site for future events.

THE ADVENTUREDOME

THE STRATOSPHERE

2000 Las Vegas Blvd S ☎ 702 380 7777, ⓦ stratospherehotel.com. Tower Mon–Thurs & Sun 10am–1am, Fri & Sat 10am–2am. $20, discounts for guests. MAP P.70, POCKET MAP L2

At 1149ft, the **Stratosphere** makes a conveniently colossal landmark to denote the northern limit of the Strip, even if strictly speaking it's located in the city proper, a full mile north of Circus Circus, its nearest active neighbour. It took quite a feat of engineering to build the tallest structure west of the Mississippi in the shifting sands of Nevada; quite amazingly, its foundations are a mere 12ft deep.

Served by Deuce buses, but not the city's Monorail system, the Stratosphere holds nothing for sightseers apart from the **Stratosphere Tower** itself. Two observation decks, one outdoors at the very summit and the other indoors on the floor below, offer fabulous views over the city and hold fascinating displays explaining everything you can see. Most visitors are up here strictly for kicks, however, to dice with death on the array of **Thrill Rides** at the very top.

STRATOSPHERE THRILL RIDES

Stratosphere, 2000 Las Vegas Blvd S ☎ 702 380 7711, ⓦ stratospherehotel.com. Mon–Thurs & Sun 11am–1am, Fri & Sat 11am–2am. X-Scream, Big Shot & Insanity: one ride (inc tower) $25, two $30, three $35, unlimited rides $40, SkyJump $120, minimum age 14. MAP P.70, POCKET MAP L2

The top of the Stratosphere serves as the launching point for several terrifying **thrill rides**, for daredevils only. **X-Scream** is a sort of giant boat that tips upside down a thousand feet above the Strip; **Insanity** is a crane that spins riders out over the abyss; **Big Shot** is a glorified sofa that free falls a couple of hundred feet. Worst of all is the **SkyJump**, in which harnessed jumpers step off a platform to fall 855ft.

Another one bites the dust

Yet another veteran fixture vanished from the Strip skyline in the summer of 2016, with the controlled explosion of the Riviera's one surviving tower, a year after the casino finally closed its doors after six decades. When built in 1955, by a consortium ranging from mobsters to the Marx Brothers, it was the Strip's first high-rise resort, designed to evoke French Mediterranean glamour; with nine storeys, it was also home to the Strip's first elevator.

During the last decade or so, as neighbours like the Stardust, the Westward Ho, and Silver City were, one by one, blasted into oblivion, the Riviera's neon starburst facade had remained a welcome flash of colour on the North Strip. It was always a losing battle, though, and it's a sign of the times that it was ultimately purchased not by a casino operator, but by the Las Vegas Convention & Visitors Authority, which paid a reported $182.5 million to make room for a proposed expansion of the city's **Convention Center**.

Shops

BONANZA GIFTS

2440 Las Vegas Blvd S ☎ 702 385 7359,
ⓦ www.worldslargestgiftshop.com. Daily
9am–9pm. MAP P.70, POCKET MAP L3

The self-proclaimed "World's
Largest Gift Shop", where
Sahara Avenue meets the
Strip, is *the* place to buy Las
Vegas souvenirs. Trinkets
celebrating the city, old and
new, include countless
variations on the iconic
"Welcome to Fabulous Las
Vegas" sign and memorabilia
from individual casinos, such
as packs of used playing cards.

FASHION SHOW

3200 Las Vegas Blvd S ☎ 702 369 8332,
ⓦ www.thefashionshow.com. Mon–Sat
10am–9pm, Sun 11am–7pm. MAP P.70,
POCKET MAP G2

The only stand-alone shopping
mall on the Strip, and for most
Las Vegas visitors the only
serious rival to in-casino malls
such as the Forum, the Fashion
Show spreads through two
two-storey buildings across from
Wynn Las Vegas. Despite the
eye-catching circular sculpture
that dangles over the pavement,
it's in no sense an attraction,
simply a functional shopping
destination. Unlike its Strip
rivals, it's large enough to hold
department stores including
Macy's, Sak's Fifth Avenue,
Nordstrom and Dillard's, as well
as an Apple Store and the usual
clothing chains.

GRAND CANAL SHOPPES

Second Level, Venetian, 3377 Las Vegas Blvd S
☎ 702 414 4525, ⓦ www.thegrandcanalshoppes
.com. Mon–Thurs & Sun 10am–11pm, Fri & Sat
10am–midnight. MAP P.70, POCKET MAP K5

Arrayed along the waterfront
upstairs in the Venetian, the
Grand Canal Shoppes may
surpass Caesars' Forum for
sheer chutzpah, but as a
shopping destination the mall
is not a serious match. It does
hold a handful of clothing
chains, such as Hugo Boss, but
consists largely of souvenir
and impulse-purchase stores,
with a big emphasis on showy
jewellery. After all, this was
where Michael Jackson went on
the celebrated million-dollar
shopping spree that's recorded
in Martin Bashir's 2003 TV
documentary about the star.

SHOPPES AT THE PALAZZO

Second Level, Palazzo, 3325 Las Vegas Blvd S
☎ 702 414 4525, ⓦ www.thegrandcanalshoppes
.com. Mon–Thurs & Sun 10am–11pm, Fri & Sat
10am–midnight. MAP P.70, POCKET MAP K5

More in keeping with the smart
stores of Wynn Las Vegas next
door than the gimmicky tone
of the nearby Grand Canal, the
Shoppes at the Palazzo are
scattered around the resort's
second floor. Few casual
visitors pass this way, so the
atmosphere tends to be hushed.
Exclusive fashion boutiques
include Jimmy Choo and
Diane von Furstenberg, and
there are also several expensive
jewellery outlets.

FASHION SHOW

COTTON ON

WYNN ESPLANADE

scallop ceviche and sushi rolls. While serious foodies will always prefer a real restaurant, if you've got a large appetite or are in a group with varying tastes, you won't be disappointed.

CRAVINGS

Mirage, 3400 Las Vegas Blvd S ☎ 702 791 7111, ⓦ mirage.com. Breakfast Mon–Fri 7–11am $19; brunch Mon–Fri 11am–3pm $24, Sat & Sun 8am–3pm $34; dinner daily 3–9pm, $31. MAP P.70, POCKET MAP F4

With its contemporary design aesthetic – rare indeed for a Las Vegas buffet, and resembling some futuristic space-age diner – *Cravings* is on a smaller scale than most of its rivals. Where possible, dishes such as stir-fries or omelettes are cooked to order; others are beautifully presented on gleaming platters. This is still mass catering – but it's a good option for a quick meal.

Restaurants

BOUCHON

Level 10, Venezia Tower, Venetian, 3355 Las Vegas Blvd S ☎ 702 414 6200, ⓦ bouchon bistro.com. Mon–Fri 7am–1pm & 5–10pm, Sat & Sun 7am–2pm & 5–10pm. MAP P.70, POCKET MAP H4

Thomas Keller's scrupulous evocation of a French bistro, hidden away on the tenth floor of the Venetian's Venezia tower, may not have novelty value, but it's a lovely, relaxed spot, with plentiful outdoor seating and food that's nothing short of *magnifique*. Brunch is the best value, with sandwiches or quiche for around $20; dinner mains like *steak frites* or *sole meunière* cost $37.

DELMONICO

Casino Level, Venetian, 3355 Las Vegas Blvd S ☎ 702 414 3737, ⓦ www.venetian .com. Mon–Thurs & Sun 11.30am–2pm & 5–10pm, Fri & Sat 11.30am–2pm & 5–10.30pm. MAP P.70, POCKET MAP H3

WYNN AND ENCORE ESPLANADES

Wynn Las Vegas, 3131 Las Vegas Blvd S ☎ 702 770 7000, ⓦ wynnlasvegas.com. Mon–Thurs 10am–11pm, Fri & Sat 10am–midnight. MAP P.70, POCKET MAP H2 & J1

There's a separate esplanade of shops in both Wynn Las Vegas and Encore, though they're all but identical in their high-end opulence. For ordinary mortals, fashion boutiques like Alexander McQueen, Givenchy and Chloé, and watch stores like Jaeger-LeCoultre and IWC Schaffhausen, make great window shopping.

Buffets

THE BUFFET AT WYNN

Wynn Las Vegas, 3131 Las Vegas Blvd S ☎ 702 770 7000, ⓦ wynnlasvegas.com. Breakfast Mon–Fri 8am–11pm $24.50; brunch Sat & Sun 8am–3.30pm $48; lunch Mon–Fri 11am–3.30pm $27; dinner Mon–Thurs & Sun 3.30–10pm $43, Fri & Sat 3.30–10.30pm $50. MAP P.70, POCKET MAP J2

Buffets are always a high priority for Steve Wynn and at Wynn Las Vegas he's got the best buffet in town. In a plush room that oozes belle époque excess, this is buffet food at its finest, with dishes from lamb osso bucco and smoked duck salad to

Renowned for bringing New Orleans food to the nation, chef Emeril Lagasse has made the Venetian the setting for a sophisticated steakhouse with a strong contemporary flavour. While the lunch menu centres on salads ($12) and sandwiches ($18), the big guns come out in the evening, with giant juicy steaks ($50) and starters like barbecue shrimp (S20).

GRAND LUX CAFE

Casino Level, Palazzo, 3325 Las Vegas Blvd S
☎ 702 733 7411, ⓦ www.grandluxcafe.com.
Mon–Thurs & Sun 6am–2am, Fri & Sat
6am–3am. MAP P.70, POCKET MAP H3

Although it's owned by the Cheesecake Factory chain, and has itself gone national, the *Grand Lux Cafe* was originally created as a casual, but nonetheless classy, 24-hour coffee shop for the Venetian, and swiftly added this slightly smarter branch in the Palazzo. Both offer wide-ranging menus of fresh, well-prepared favourites from around the world at good prices – pizza and salad costs $12, Jamaican pork tenderloin or Yankee pot roast $19 – and have their own on-site bakeries.

LAVO

Casino Level, Palazzo, 3325 Las Vegas Blvd S
☎ 702 791 1800, ⓦ lavolv.com. Mon–Fri
5pm–midnight, Sat 10am–6pm & 7pm–
midnight, Sun 10am–4pm & 7pm–midnight.
MAP P.70, POCKET MAP H3

Considering it's attached to the exclusive *Lavo* nightclub, this is an oddly traditional Italian restaurant, dark and romantic rather than loud or brash. The food too is rich and authentic, and the prices relatively restrained, with pizzas for $22, pasta specials a little more and Mediterranean classics like veal *parmigiano* costing up to $46.

LVB BURGERS

Mirage, 3400 Las Vegas Blvd S ☎ 702 792
7888, ⓦ mirage.com. Mon–Thurs & Sun
11am–2am, Fri & Sat 11am–4am. MAP P.70,
POCKET MAP F5

So-called "gourmet burger" joints are all the rage in Las Vegas. Lively long after midnight, this one, in a former tiger pen near the front of the Mirage, serves a delicious Oh My Gosh duck burger for $16 or an Old School burger for $15, plus a zesty $18 soy-salmon burger.

PHO

TI, 3300 Las Vegas Blvd S ☎ 702 894 7111,
ⓦ treasureisland.com. Mon–Thurs & Sun
11am–11.30pm, Fri & Sat 11am–1.30am.
MAP P.73, POCKET MAP G3

You could easily fail to notice that half the time, half of TI's 24-hour *Coffee Shop* is given over to this inexpensive and excellent Vietnamese diner. The pho of the name is steaming noodle soup; prices start at $16 and increase depending on the meat or fish you add. They also serve spring rolls and dry noodle dishes, and sneak in some sushi options and Chinese favourites too.

RED 8

Wynn Las Vegas, 3131 Las Vegas Blvd S ☎ 702 770 7000, ⊛ wynnlasvegas.com. Mon–Thurs & Sun 11.30am–midnight, Fri & Sat 11.30am–1am. MAP P.70, POCKET MAP J2

This decadent, deep-red, pan-Asian restaurant makes a stylish retreat from Wynn's adjoining casino floor and serves a full menu of Chinese classics, from dim sum dumplings at $10 to chow mein or *ho fun* noodles for around $20, as well as Thai fish cakes and Malaysian satay and *laksa*.

SAMBA

Mirage, 3400 Las Vegas Blvd S ☎ 866 339 4566, ⊛ mirage.com. Mon–Thurs & Sun 5–9pm, Sat & Sun 5–10pm. MAP P.70, POCKET MAP F4

With its bright playful decor and billowing couches, open to the main walkway through the Mirage, you can't but be drawn towards this enticing, high-quality Brazilian steakhouse. Hefty meat dishes typically cost around $30, with starters like ceviche or coconut prawns more like $10, while $45 buys an all-you-can-eat feast of barbecued meats, from sirloin to turkey, plus black beans and rice.

SAMBA

SINATRA

Encore, 3121 Las Vegas Blvd S ☎ 702 770 5320, ⊛ wynnlasvegas.com. Daily 5.30–10.30pm. MAP P.70, POCKET MAP J1

The Sinatra name, licensed by Frank's family, is of course a gimmick, but it tells you what to expect – the kind of idealized Italian restaurant the Rat Pack might have frequented back in the 1960s, formal and romantic and not in the slightest bit calorie-conscious. Ol' Blue Eyes is everywhere, from the speakers to the menu, with his favourite spaghetti and clams for $34 and osso bucco "My Way" for $53.

TAO ASIAN BISTRO

Second Level, Venetian, 3355 Las Vegas Blvd S ☎ 702 388 8338, ⊛ taorestaurantlv.com. Mon–Thurs & Sun 5pm–midnight, Fri & Sat 5pm–1am. MAP P.70, POCKET MAP J5

By far the busiest and most profitable restaurant in the entire US, *Tao* is a place to come for the experience – the over-the-top opium-den decor, the giant Buddha statue, the crowds of dressed-up clubbers getting ready to party in the *Tao* nightclub next door – as much as the showy Asian food. And the food is good – pork or duck with sizzling fried rice costs $15, and steak or sea bass is around $38.

TOP OF THE WORLD

Stratosphere, 2000 Las Vegas Blvd S ☎ 702 380 7711, ⊛ topoftheworldlv.com. Lunch and dinner Mon–Thurs & Sun 11am–10.30pm, Fri & Sat 11am–11pm. MAP P.70, POCKET MAP L2

While it's a lot classier than the hotel-casino far below, this restaurant only stands out for the compelling reason that it's over 800ft up in the air, and revolves every 80 minutes to give magnificent views over the Strip. Lunchtime is the cheapest time (sandwiches $25; steaks $34), but dinner is much more romantic (mains start at $36).

WAZUZU

Bars and lounges

WAZUZU

Encore, 3121 Las Vegas Blvd S ☎ 702 770 3463, Ⓦ wynnlasvegas.com. Mon–Thurs & Sun 11.30am–10.30pm, Fr & Sat 11.30am–1am. MAP P.70, POCKET MAP J1

Approached by an avenue of six colossal gilt pears, and featuring a huge crystal dragon squirming along its back wall, Wazuzu is by far the best-looking restaurant in Encore, and it serves the best food too. As well as sushi, it draws on Asian cuisines from Korea (short ribs $25) and Mongolia (wok-tossed beef $22) to Thailand (chicken basil stir-fry $21). Be sure to try the sake too.

ZEFFIRINO

The Venetian, 3355 Las Vegas Blvd S ☎ 702 414 3500, Ⓦ www.thevenetian.com. Daily 11.30am–midnight. MAP P.70, POCKET MAP K5

Any Las Vegas aficionado must surely love the Venetian branch of this venerable Genoa restaurant, which is both romantic, with its rich tapestries, and playful, with ornate balconies overlooking the Grand Canal. Typical dinner mains like shrimp ravioli or grilled sea bass cost $30–45, but the $30 three-course set lunch (Mon–Sat) is exceptional value.

GILLEY'S SALOON

TI, 3300 Las Vegas Blvd S ☎ 702 894 7111, Ⓦ gilleyslasvegas.com. Mon–Thurs & Sun 11am–2am, Fr & Sat 11am–4am $10 cover for live bands. MAP P.70, POCKET MAP G3

This raucous country and rodeo saloon practically defines the new TI. Bikini-clad "Gilley Girls" ride the mechanical bulls, and you can join a free line-dancing lesson most nights at 7pm, drink two-for-one rum cocktails until 10pm, or dance to honky-tonk bands until long after midnight.

JAPONAIS

Mirage, 3400 Las Vegas Blvd S ☎ 866 339 4566, Ⓦ mirage.com. Mon–Thurs & Sun 5–10pm, Fri & Sat 5pm–midnight. MAP P.70, POCKET MAP F4

While the dining room at Japonais, at the heart of the Mirage, serves everything from steak to sushi, the separate lounge and bar area is a stunning, glamorous spot for pre- or after-show drinks, swathed in flowing, spotlit fabrics and offering surprisingly intimate seating areas.

PARASOL UP, PARASOL DOWN

Wynn Las Vegas, 3131 Las Vegas Blvd S ☎ 702 770 7000, Ⓦ wynnlasvegas.com. Mon–Thurs & Sun 11am–4am, Fri & Sat 11am–5am. MAP P.70, POCKET MAP J2

A quintessential example of the Wynn way with design, these twin upstairs-downstairs bars, festooned with richly coloured umbrellas and filling Wynn's central stairway, are the perfect place to admire the Lake of Dreams. A cocktail or two, and you'll feel right at Las Vegas's absurd and exhilarating heart.

PEPPERMILL FIRESIDE LOUNGE

PEPPERMILL FIRESIDE LOUNGE

2985 Las Vegas Blvd S ☎ 702 735 4177,
🖵 peppermilllasvegas.com. Daily 24hr.
MAP P.70, POCKET MAP B11

A magnificent relic from
the glory days, somehow
surviving on the North Strip
just north of Encore, this
wonderful Vegas veteran
outclasses any of the casino
lounges with its pink neon,
mirrored walls and central
flame-spouting fire pit, and a
spectacular assortment of
colourful cocktails, culminating
in its signature 64oz Scorpion.
The attached diner serves an
appropriately retro-flavoured
food menu, from ham-and-egg
breakfasts to pineapple-topped
burgers and dinner steaks.

SEÑOR FROG'S

TI, 3300 Las Vegas Blvd S ☎ 702 894 7777,
🖵 senorfrogs.com. Mon–Thurs & Sun
midnight–2am, Fri & Sat 11am–4am. MAP P.70,
POCKET MAP G3

This totally raucous, hugely
enjoyable indoor-outdoor
Mexican-themed bar overlooks
what used to be the pirate
lagoon outside Treasure Island,
and with its enormous open-air
deck it makes a great spot for a
sunset margarita or after-hours
cocktail. As well as live bands
on Fridays, they have a drag
brunch every Saturday,
followed by a Latin night.

Clubs and
music venues

1 OAK

Mirage, 3400 Las Vegas Blvd S ☎ 702 588
5656, 🖵 1oaklasvegas.com. Wed, Fri &
Sat 10.30pm–4am. Cover varies. MAP P.70,
POCKET MAP F4

An offshoot of the New York
original, the Mirage's glitzy
hip-hop nightclub – the name
stands for "One Of A Kind"
– is renowned for high-profile
guest appearances, including
a New Year's Eve DJ set by
Kanye West. Decorated with
zebra-stripe flooring and a
dozen artworks by Roy
Nachum, it's capable of holding
well over a thousand people.
Each of its two separate rooms
has its own DJ booth, but most
of the tables are reserved for
patrons prepared to pay high
prices for bottle service.

ENCORE BEACH CLUB

Encore, 3121 Las Vegas Blvd S ☎ 702 770
7300, 🖵 www.encorebeachclub.com. Late April
to Oct Thurs & Sat 10am–7pm, Fri & Sun 11am–
7pm. Cover $20–60. MAP P.70, POCKET MAP J1

This luxurious multilevel
complex of pools, patios, bars
and private bungalows, in front
of Encore but still thoroughly
screened from the Strip, has to
be the definitive expression of
Las Vegas's recent craze for
DJ-fuelled daytime poolside
parties. No money could buy the
worldwide publicity it received
as the scene of Prince Harry
Windsor's notorious antics in
2012, so not surprisingly it's now
even more packed than ever.

Exhausted revellers can escape the crowds either on pristine white "lily pads" out in the water or in private cabanas, but the pounding music will follow you everywhere. Expect to pay ultra-high prices even for regular drinks, let alone table service.

SURRENDER

Encore, 3121 Las Vegas Blvd S ☎ 702 770 3300, ⊕ surrendernightclub.com. Wed, Fri & Sat 10.30pm–4am. Cover men $30, women $20. MAP P.70, POCKET MAP J1

The opulent indoor-outdoor complex that's home in summer to the daytime beach club is much too good to leave empty. Instead it opens at night year-round, with DJs playing poolside, pole dancers cavorting, and drinks prices soaring like skyrockets. Wednesday is "industry" – ie locals' – night, while the big names appear at weekends.

TAO

Second Level, Venetian, 3355 Las Vegas Blvd S ☎ 702 388 8338, ⊕ taolasvegas.com. Nightclub Thurs–Sat 10pm–5am; Tao Beach late April to Oct daily 10am–sunset. Cover Thurs & Fri $20, Sat $40 weekend wristband $100. MAP P.70, POCKET MAP J5

An immediate hit in 2005 and still very much the place to be seen, this dynamic high-concept Asian-style nightclub inevitably attracts larger crowds than its small dance floor can handle. Even on the guest list you'll have to wait to get in and you'll pay heavily for any private space. The open-air *Tao Beach* pool club is a great place to gear up for the evening. Weekend wristbands also give admission to the same owners' *Lavo* club in the adjacent Palazzo.

XS

Encore, 3121 Las Vegas Blvd S ☎ 702 521 4005, ⊕ www.xslasvegas.com. Mon 10.30pm–4am, Fri & Sat 10pm–4am. Cover $20–30, men $50 Sat. MAP P.70, POCKET MAP J1

Where do Encore's beautiful people go when they've had enough pool time at the beach club? To the even more decadent *XS* nightclub, of course, to stay in the tropical mood, throw some moves on the massive dancefloor, and drink some very classy cocktails.

ENCORE BEACH CLUB

Shows

HUMAN NATURE

Venetian, 3355 Las Vegas Blvd S ☎ 702 414 9000, ⓦ www.humannaturelive.com. Tues–Sat 7pm. $67–121. MAP P.70, POCKET MAP H4

Having enjoyed huge success with their own material back home, this wholesome Australian vocal quartet moved to Las Vegas, where their show proved enough of a smash to transfer from the (now defunct) Imperial Palace to the Venetian in 2013. Their unlikely Stateside mission, to add a down-under twist to the Motown sound, enjoys the personal blessing of Smokey Robinson himself. And no wonder – with their fabulous voices and very likeable energy, they really are superb. A smokin' live band plays the music, and the boys simply soar.

LE RÊVE

Wynn Las Vegas, 3131 Las Vegas Blvd S ☎ 702 770 9966, ⓦ wynnlasvegas.com. Mon, Tues & Fri–Sun 7pm & 9.30pm. $115–175. MAP P.70, POCKET MAP J2

Le Rêve – "The Dream" – is also the title of Steve Wynn's favourite personal Picasso and

was the working name of his casino too. For the show itself, Wynn dreamed of hiring former Cirque du Soleil talent to out-Cirque Cirque with an even more unbelievable extravaganza of colour and spectacle, featuring more water than O and wilder costumes than Mystère. In terms of sheer looks it succeeds, with astonishing coups de théâtre; you'll need to overlook the vacuity of the plot, though, in which the endlessly bemused protagonist dreams of finding "the answer to life".

LOVE

Mirage, 3400 Las Vegas Blvd S ☎ 702 792 7777, ⓦ cirquedusoleil.com. Mon & Thurs–Sat 7pm & 9.30pm, Sun 7pm. $126–182. MAP P.70, POCKET MAP F5

A genuinely triumphant collaboration between Cirque du Soleil and the Beatles, in which Cirque perform superbly choreographed dancing and acrobatics to a crystal-sharp Beatles soundtrack, Love is much, much more than just another "jukebox musical". There's no story and no attempt to depict the Beatles as actual people – though eerily we hear their voices in retrieved studio chatter – just a dazzling celebration of their music and the times and places that made them who they were.

MYSTÈRE

TI, 3300 Las Vegas Blvd S ☎ 702 894 7722, ⓦ cirquedusoleil.com. Mon–Wed, Sat & Sun 7pm & 9.30pm. $75–136. MAP P.70, POCKET MAP G3

Twenty-five years since it first opened at Treasure Island, Las Vegas's original Cirque du Soleil show is still arguably the best – you can see why it changed the Strip's entertainment scene forever, overnight. Mystère is pure spectacle, from its gorgeous costumes and

LOVE

billows of cascading silk to its jaw-dropping circus skills and phenomenal feats of strength.

TERRY FATOR

Mirage, 3400 Las Vegas Blvd S ☎ 702 792 7777, ⓦ mirage.com Mon–Thurs 7.30pm. $61–100. MAP P.70, POCKET MAP F4

Yes, this middle-American ventriloquist swaps corny jokes with soft-toy puppets, but he also has an extraordinary talent: an astonishing five-octave singing voice that delivers perfect impressions of artists from Ozzy Osbourne to Etta James – all without moving his lips. Despite rocketing to fame and fortune since he won *America's Got Talent* in 2007, he is still likeable and down-to-earth.

Wedding chapels

CHAPEL OF THE BELLS

2233 Las Vegas Blvd S ☎ 702 735 6803, ⓦ chapelofthebellslasvegas.com. Mon–Thurs & Sun 9am–9pm, Fri & Sat 9am–midnight. MAP P.70, POCKET MAP L3

Crammed up against the singularly unprepossessing

Fun City Motel, just north of Sahara Avenue, this little chapel conceals a romantic heart beneath its garish exterior. Draped in white silk, with the sun streaming in, it's really quite attractive – and if it was good enough for Pele, it's good enough for you. Non-denominational weddings start at $175; pay $255 or more and you get free transport to and from your hotel plus a DVD of the service.

CHAPEL OF THE FLOWERS

1717 Las Vegas Blvd S ☎ 702 735 4331, ⓦ littlechapel.com. Mon–Thurs 9am–8pm, Fri & Sat 9am–10pm. MAP P.70, POCKET MAP M1

With three separate chapels opening onto the same garden and couples queuing to take snaps at the waterfall, things can get a bit hectic at peak times, but in principle it's all surprisingly tasteful. Most popular is the Victorian chapel, with its marble floors and mahogany pews. Packages, categorized as Intimate, Elegant or Legendary, range from $495 to $9000.

A LITTLE WHITE WEDDING CHAPEL

1301 Las Vegas Blvd S ☎ 702 382 5943, ⓦ www.alittlewhitechapel.com. Daily 8am–midnight. MAP P.70, POCKET MAP L4

The definitive only-in-Vegas wedding chapel, as used by Joan Collins and Michael Jordan, not to mention Britney, has grown and grown to include five separate chapels. Four resemble reasonably pleasant areas in, say, a chain hotel; the fifth, the notorious "Tunnel of Love", is basically the former driveway, roofed over with angels painted on the ceiling, and hosts drive-through weddings from as little as $75 (bring your own car).

Downtown Las Vegas

Amounting, as far as visitors are concerned, to little more than three or four blocks, downtown is where Las Vegas started out when the railroad arrived in 1905, and also held its first casinos back in the 1930s. Many visitors prefer downtown to the Strip, feeling that by offering serious gambling, plus cheap bars, restaurants and buffets, its no-nonsense casinos represent the "real" Las Vegas. With its old-style neon signs and garish arrays of multicoloured light bulbs, it also looks much more like the Las Vegas of popular imagination than the high-tech Strip, while in the artificial sky of the Fremont Street Experience canopy it boasts a genuine must-see attraction. What's more, thanks to revitalization efforts that include the opening of the intriguing Mob Museum and the highbrow Smith Center arts centre, downtown finally appears to be on the way back up again.

FREMONT STREET EXPERIENCE

Fremont St, between Main and Fourth sts
☎ 702 678 5777, ⓦ vegasexperience.com.
Nightly, on the hour from sunset until 1am.
Free. MAP P.87, POCKET MAP G12

Wanting to give downtown a large-scale spectacle to match the Strip and make visitors feel safer outdoors at night, the downtown casinos came up with an amazing rebranding scheme – they put a roof over four city blocks and renamed downtown the **Fremont Street Experience**. After dark, the sky itself seems to become a giant movie screen – a dazzling light show of monsters and mayhem. Live bands pump out rock classics on stages set up at the main intersections – typically tribute acts to the likes of Bon Jovi or the Doors – and downtown parties until long after midnight.

FREMONT STREET EXPERIENCE

Downtown Las Vegas

MAIN STREET STATION

CALIFORNIA

THE PLAZA

THE GOLDEN GATE

BINION'S GAMBLING HALL

FREMONT HOTEL

Fremont Street Experience

Greyhound Station

GOLDEN NUGGET

FOUR QUEENS

THE D

The Mob Museum

DOWNTOWN GRAND

Neonopolis

SlotZilla

EL CORTEZ

EAST STEWART AVENUE

EAST OGDEN AVENUE

FREMONT STREET

CARSON AVENUE

BRIDGER AVENUE

LEWIS AVE

LEWIS AVENUE

EAST CLARK AVENUE

EAST BONNEVILLE AVENUE

CITY PARKWAY

Disused railway

SOUTH MAIN STREET

SOUTH 1ST STREET

SOUTH CASINO CENTER BOULEVARD

N. CASINO CENTER AVENUE

SOUTH 3RD STREET

SOUTH 4TH STREET

LAS VEGAS BOULEVARD SOUTH (THE STRIP)

NORTH 4TH ST

LAS VEGAS BLVD NORTH

NORTH 6TH ST

0 metres 200
0 yards 200

Neon Museum & Las Vegas Natural History Museum (900 yards)

(550 yards)

LAS VEGAS HOSTEL (800 yards)

Bonneville Transit Center

Graceland Wedding Chapel

BARS & LOUNGES	
Art Bar	2
Chicago Brewing Co	4
Downtown Cocktail Room	6
The Griffin	5
Triple 7 Restaurant and Microbrewery	1
MUSIC VENUE	
Smith Center for the Performing Arts	3

BUFFETS	
Golden Nugget Buffet	5
Paradise Buffet and Café	4
RESTAURANTS	
Hash House A Go Go	1
Oscar's Beef * Booze * Broads	3
Second Street Grill	6
Triple George Grill	2

SHOPS	
Gamblers General Store	1
Las Vegas Premium Outlets (North)	2

SLOTZILLA

Fremont St ☎ 702 678 5780.
🌐 vegasexperience.com. Mon–Thurs & Sun 1pm–1am; Fri & Sat 1pm–2am. Zipline $25. Zoomline $45. Weight restrictions apply.
MAP P.87, POCKET MAP G12

Unveiled in 2013, **SlotZilla** is an extraordinary two-tier zip line centring on the world's biggest slot machine. The 120ft-tall monstrosity ejects four riders at a time on each level. The lower Zipline has seats; riders on the upper Zoomline fly like Superman through the canopy of the Fremont Street Experience.

THE PLAZA

1 Main St ☎ 702 386 2110, 🌐 www.plaza hotelcasino.com. MAP P.87, POCKET MAP F11

Once Las Vegas's railroad station, the huge **Plaza** casino looked set to shut up shop in 2010. Surprisingly, it reopened within a year following a $35 million face-lift. Its owners cannily bought up the furnishings of the abandoned Fontainebleu, and the re-vamped Plaza now holds some of downtown's best bars and restaurants, including Oscar Goodman's glass-domed steakhouse (see p.92).

THE GOLDEN GATE

1 E Fremont St ☎ 702 385 1906, 🌐 golden gatecasino.com. MAP P.87, POCKET MAP G11

Having opened in 1906, the **Golden Gate** is only a year younger than the city itself. A railroad hotel before becoming a casino, it still has only a hundred rooms and remains an appealing historical anomaly. Recent modernizations have stripped away some of its charms, however, including the 99¢ shrimp cocktail bar; they're now $2.99 from the 24-hour bakery.

GOLDEN NUGGET

129 E Fremont St ☎ 702 385 7111, Ⓦ goldennugget.com/lasvegas. MAP P.87, POCKET MAP G12

Downtown's largest and highest-profile casino, the **Golden Nugget** has more in common with the Strip than with its neighbours. Built in 1946, it's among the city's oldest casinos, but its current incarnation owes more to the 1970s, when it was acquired by a young man who was to become the leading entrepreneur of modern Las Vegas: Steve Wynn. Downtown has traditionally been characterized by "sawdust joints"; Wynn gave the Golden Nugget the bright, glittery feel it retains to this day.

The most visible result of remodelling by its latest owners is the open-air swimming pool at its heart; guests who plummet down its towering waterslide pass in a clear tube through a shark-filled aquarium. Most recently, the casino opened up its Fremont Street facade, adding *Bar 46* to create a prime vantage point for the light show on Fremont Street. The casino holds little for sightseers other than an actual golden nugget; the 62-pound, million-dollar Hand of Faith was found in Australia in 1980.

BINION'S GAMBLING HALL

128 E Fremont St ☎ 702 382 1600, Ⓦ www .binions.com. MAP P.87, POCKET MAP G12

If you think owning a casino is a sure-fire way to make money, **Binion's Gambling Hall** offers a salutary lesson. When its original owner, Benny Binion, died in 1989, this was, as Binion's Horseshoe, Las Vegas's most profitable casino. His heirs ran the place so badly that it lost its rooms and even its name. Caesars Entertainment briefly bought it to acquire the Horseshoe name and the World Series of Poker, but sold it on.

Binion's today is in a sorry state, with big empty spaces devoid even of slot machines. Its one gimmick is that visitors can pose for free photos with a million dollars in cash; it takes half an hour to get your print.

FOUR QUEENS

202 E Fremont St ☎ 702 385 4011, Ⓦ www .fourqueens.com. MAP P.87, POCKET MAP G12

Opened in 1966 and named for its owner's four daughters, the **Four Queens** fills a whole block of Fremont Street. Its basic role is to soak up any spillover from the Golden Nugget; it holds little apart from a decent pub, the *Chicago Brewing Company* and the *Canyon Club* showroom/nightclub.

GOLDEN NUGGET

FREMONT HOTEL

200 E Fremont St ☎ 702 385 3232, ⓦ www
.fremontcasino.com. MAP F.37, POCKET MAP G12

Ranking a distant second behind
the Golden Nugget in terms
of glitz and glamour, but still
ahead of its other downtown
neighbours, the **Fremont Hotel**
is a smart but otherwise
unremarkable casino. Back in
1956 this was Nevada's tallest
building; now it's noteworthy
as the home of above-par
restaurants, and little else.

THE D

301 E Fremont St ☎ 702 388 2400,
ⓦ www.thed.com. MAP P.87 POCKET MAP G12

A rare example of a casino
completely changing both its
image and its name, **The D** was
until a few years ago a fake-Irish
joint called Fitzgeralds, guarded
by Mr O'Lucky the leprechaun.
The "D" stands for downtown
and Detroit, hometown of
owner, Derek Stevens. He's taken
advantage of the most unusual
feature, that the casino has two
storeys, to give each a different
character – a contemporary style
at street level, where go-go
dancers gyrate in the "party pit",
and vintage upstairs. Entertainment includes live music and
comedy, plus a murder-mystery
dinner theatre.

EL CORTEZ

600 E Fremont St ☎ 702 385 5200, ⓦ elcortez
hotelcasino.com. MAP P.87, POCKET MAP H12

Long celebrated as downtown's
most cheerfully downmarket
casino, the seventy-year-old
El Cortez is looking remarkably
spruce thanks to a freshly
remodelled facade. For a taste
of days gone by, as well as cheap
dining and some of the best
gambling odds around, it's worth
braving the slightly intimidating
five-minute walk east of the
Fremont Street Experience even
if you're not staying here.

EL CORTEZ

MAIN STREET STATION

200 N Main St ☎ 702 387 1896, ⓦ www
.mainstreetcasino.com. MAP P.87, POCKET MAP G11

At a little over twenty years old,
Main Street Station, just north
of the Plaza, is downtown's
youngest major casino. Despite
its antique-filled Victoriana
theme, it's also among the
brightest casinos. While it
doesn't belong to the Station
chain ubiquitous elsewhere in
the city, it offers a similar range
of restaurants and bars.

THE NEON MUSEUM

770 Las Vegas Blvd N ☎ 702 387 6366,
ⓦ www.neonmuseum.org. Tours daily from
10am onwards; precise schedules vary. Day
tours $19; after-dark tours $25. MAP P.87,
POCKET MAP H10

If your appetite is whetted by
the vintage signs displayed
along Fremont Street, east of
Las Vegas Boulevard, take a
tour of the **Neon Museum** half
a mile north. Treasuring signs
and sculptures salvaged from
long-lost casinos like the
Desert Inn and the Hacienda,
this is basically a junkyard,
without even restrooms. Come
after dark to see it at its best.
The visitor centre was once
the space-age lobby of *La
Concha Motel.*

THE MOB MUSEUM

300 Stewart Ave ☎ 702 229 2734, ⊛ themob
museum.org. Daily 9am–9pm. $24, ages 11–17
$14, under-11s free. MAP P.87, POCKET MAP G11

Opened on February 14, 2012, the 83rd anniversary of the Saint Valentine's Day Massacre, Las Vegas's **Mob Museum** was designed as the lynchpin of a campaign by then-mayor Oscar Goodman – a former lawyer who defended many underworld figures – to revitalize downtown as a tourist destination. Its full name, the National Museum of Organized Crime and Law Enforcement, reflects its dual goal of chronicling the mobsters who once controlled the city and the lawmen who eventually brought them down.

The museum takes up three storeys of the imposing former federal courthouse, two blocks north of Fremont Street. One upstairs courtroom has been restored to how it looked in 1950 when it hosted hearings by Senator Estes' Senate committee investigating organized crime.

With its comprehensive displays giving the inside stories on all sorts of Las Vegas characters and conspiracies, the Mob Museum is a fascinating place to spend a few hours. It likes to pitch itself as offering a serious perspective on the city's entanglement with the underworld; however, it has a disconcerting propensity for trivializing or glamorizing Las Vegas's gangster past. Lurid panels detail, for example, the "Mob's Greatest Hits", while waxworks depict gory corpses.

DISCOVERY CHILDREN'S MUSEUM

360 Promenade Place ☎ 702 382 5437,
⊛ www.discoverykidslv.org. June–Sept Mon–Sat
10am–5pm, Sun noon–5pm; Oct–May Tues–Fri
9am–4pm, Sat 10am–5pm, Sun noon–5pm;
ages 1–99 $14.50. MAP P.87, POCKET MAP F12

Safely ensconced in spacious new premises, next to the Smith Center half a mile west of Fremont Street, the long-established **Discovery Children's Museum** remains a favourite with younger children in particular. Centring on the three-storey indoor Summit Tower, with twelve levels of interactive science exhibits, it also holds play areas such as a medieval castle.

LAS VEGAS NATURAL HISTORY MUSEUM

900 Las Vegas Blvd N ☎ 702 384 3466,
⊛ lvnhm.org. Daily 9am–4pm. $10, ages 3–11
$5. MAP P.87, POCKET MAP H10

Collections at the **Las Vegas Natural History Museum**, a mile north of downtown, range from stuffed lions to anima-tronic dinosaurs, complemented by tanks of live sharks and snakes. One remarkable specimen, a dinosaur that was naturally mummified before it became a fossil, prompts an intriguing CSI-style investiga-tion into its life and death. There's also a replica of Tutankhamun's tomb, donated by the Luxor when it stripped away its former Egyptian theme.

LAS VEGAS NATURAL HISTORY MUSEUM

Shops

GAMBLERS GENERAL STORE

800 S Main St ☎ 702 382 9903, ⓦ www
.gamblersgeneralstore.com. Mon–Sat 9am–6pm,
Sun 9am–5pm. MAP P.87, POCKET MAP F13

If you love gambling, but
sometimes wish you got
something back for your
money, this is the place to
come. You can buy anything
from a $1.99 pack of playing
cards used at your favourite
casino to a $3600 roulette
wheel, strategy books and
non-gaming souvenirs.

GAMBLERS GENERAL STORE

LAS VEGAS PREMIUM OUTLETS (NORTH)

875 S Grand Central Parkway ☎ 702 366 9015,
ⓦ premiumoutlets.com. Mon–Sat 9am–9pm,
Sun 9am–8pm. MAP P.87, POCKET MAP F13

A mile west of downtown and
served by SDX buses (see p.125)
from the Strip, this huge mall
consists of over 150 stores
accessed via outdoor walkways.
Unlike the south-Strip branch
(see p.38), most are genuinely
"outlets" of well-known brands
– Diesel, Tommy Hilfiger, Nike
– so you can find real bargains.

Buffets

GOLDEN NUGGET BUFFET

Golden Nugget, 129 E Fremont St ☎ 702
385 7111, ⓦ goldennugget.com/lasvegas.
Breakfast Mon–Fri 7–10.30am, $16;
champagne brunch Sat & Sun 7am–3.30pm
$23; lunch Mon–Fri 10.30am–3.30pm $17;
dinner daily 3.30–10pm Mon–Wed $23,
Thurs & Sat $25, Fri $27, Sun $27. MAP P.87,
POCKET MAP G12

As you might expect of a
casino once owned by Steve
Wynn, the Golden Nugget
boasts downtown's best buffet,
offering various cuisines in a
humdrum space. The weekend
"seafood and more" dinners
are the best bargain.

PARADISE BUFFET AND CAFÉ

Fremont Hotel, 200 Fremont St ☎ 702 385
3232, ⓦ www.fremontcasino.com. Breakfast
Mon–Fri 7–10.30am, $8.50; champagne
brunch Sat & Sun 7am–3pm, $13.50; lunch
Mon–Fri 11am–3pm, $9.50; dinner Mon–Thurs
& Sun 4–10pm, Fri & Sat 4–11pm, Mon,
Wed, Thurs, Sat & Sun $15.50, Tues & Fri $22.
MAP P.87, POCKET MAP G12

Downtown has always been
popular with Hawaiian visitors,
and with palm trees and bright
colours, the Fremont's buffet
gives a taste of the islands
themselves. The food concen-
trates on American classics;
prices go up for the "Seafood
Fantasy" (Tues and Fri). There is
also a separate café menu.

Restaurants

HASH HOUSE A GO GO

The Plaza, 1 Main St ☎ 702 386 4646,
ⓦ hashhouseagogo.com/vegas. Mon–Thurs
& Sun 7am–11pm, Fri & Sat 7am–midnight.
MAP P.87, POCKET MAP F11

This gleaming, all-day diner is
hardly the place for a romantic
rendezvous, but its "twisted farm
food" – obscenely large portions
of wholesome American country
classics like pot pie – tastes good
and is great value. It's best for
breakfast, with a varied menu.

OSCAR'S BEEF * BOOZE * BROADS

The Plaza, 1 Main St ☏ 702 386 7227,
ⓦ www.oscarslv.com. Daily 5–10pm. MAP P.87,
POCKET MAP F11

Perched in a glass bubble
overlooking Fremont Street, this
shameless bid by former mayor
Oscar Goodman to cash in on
his larger-than-life image is a
favourite with all who fondly
remember the old Las Vegas.
A New York-style steakhouse,
serving quality filet mignon or
bone-in steaks ($40-plus), it also
has an Italian-heavy menu. The
"broads" are the hostesses, who
can also be hired as dinner
companions.

SECOND STREET GRILL

Fremont Hotel, 200 E Fremont St ☏ 702 385
3232, ⓦ www.fremontcasino.com. Wed, Thurs
& Sun 5–10pm, Fri & Sat 5–11pm. MAP P.87,
POCKET MAP G12

Despite its dreary, windowless
setting, this gourmet restaurant
offers downtown's most
inventive cuisine. Asian-
influenced fish dishes like
the tuna sashimi starter or
sesame-crusted *mahi-mahi*
reflect its Hawaiian roots,
while dishes like chicken breast
with risotto and pesto are also
on offer. Mains cost $25-plus,
while the nightly special
T-bone dinner is $30.

TRIPLE GEORGE GRILL

201 N Third St ☏ 702 384 2761, ⓦ triple
georgegrill.com. Mon–Thurs 11am–11pm,
Fri 11am–midnight, Sat 4pm–midnight, Sun
4–11pm. MAP P.87, POCKET MAP G11

Its speakeasy decor, mixing
brickwork with wood
panelling, might not be
genuine, but this downtown
steakhouse is a real hangout
for local politicos and lawyers.
Come early for lunch and
watch them wheeling and
dealing in the back room over
$14 Caesar salads, $14 chicken
fettuccini or $19 steaks.

Bars and lounges

ART BAR

201 N Third St ☏ 702 719 5100,
ⓦ downtowngrand.com. Mon–Thurs & Sun
3–11pm, Fri & Sat 4pm–midnight. MAP P.87,
POCKET MAP G11

Just off the lobby of the
Downtown Grand – formerly
the Lady Luck – the *Art Bar*
lives up to its name by
festooning its ceiling with
artworks. Happy Hour (5–7pm)
is the ideal time to relax over a
cocktail in its plush armchairs,
perhaps after visiting the Mob
Museum opposite.

CHICAGO BREWING CO

Four Queens, 202 E Fremont St ☏ 702 924
5222, ⓦ www.fourqueens.com. Mon–Fri
11.30am–1.30am, Sat & Sun 10am–1.30am.
MAP P.87, POCKET MAP G12

Fremont Street's best bar and
the pick of Las Vegas's few
microbreweries is a noisy and
upbeat spot to enjoy American,
German and English-style
beers, brewed on site and sold
individually or in 64-oz, $15
"Growlers". They also serve
pizzas, wings and sandwiches.

TRIPLE GEORGE GRILL

DOWNTOWN COCKTAIL ROOM

111 Las Vegas Blvd S ☎ 702 880 3696,
ⓦ thedowntownlv.com. Mon–Fri 4pm–2am,
Sat 7pm–2am. MAP P.87, POCKET MAP G12

Aimed at in-the-know locals
rather than tourists, this small,
dimly lit cocktail lounge,
tucked away behind an
industrial facade, evokes
downtown's long-lost glory
days. Expert mixologists create
classic and original cocktails
($10–14), plus there's an early
evening bar menu and live DJs
after 9pm (Wed–Sat).

THE GRIFFIN

511 Fremont St ☎ 702 382 0577. Mon–Sat
5pm–3am, Sun 9pm–3am. MAP P.87,
POCKET MAP G12

This cavernous downtown bar
is just a short walk from the
main cluster of casinos, beyond
the Fremont Street Experience,
but it's a world away from the
downtown norm. In-the-know
locals, including a strong
hipster contingent, weave
through the black velvet curtain
guarding the entrance to settle
down by the fireside or find a
private booth. Everything turns
a bit more hectic at weekends,
when local bands or DJs strut
their stuff in the back room.

TRIPLE 7 RESTAURANT AND MICROBREWERY

Main Street Station, 200 N Main St ☎ 702
386 4442, ⓦ www.mainstreetcasino.com. Daily
11am–7am. MAP P.87, POCKET MAP G11

This cavernous pub and
restaurant, at the heart of the
antique-filled casino, is always
full of lively, cheery drinkers
savouring European brews
and substantial portions of
good pub grub.

Venue

SMITH CENTER FOR THE PERFORMING ARTS

361 Symphony Park Ave ☎ 702 749 2000,
ⓦ www.thesmithcenter.com. See website for
programme and prices. MAP P.87, POCKET MAP F12

Las Vegas acquired a
performing arts centre in
2012 with the opening of this
showpiece Art Deco-influenced
theatre half a mile west of
downtown. Its two-thousand-
seat auditorium hosts classical
concerts, ballet and touring
Broadway shows, while smaller
showrooms put on a varied
programme of live music
and theatre.

Wedding chapel

GRACELAND WEDDING CHAPEL

619 S Las Vegas Blvd ☎ 702 382 0091,
ⓦ www.gracelandchapel.com. Daily
9am–11pm. MAP P.87, POCKET MAP G13

This pretty chapel, just south
of downtown, is "the home of
the original Elvis wedding".
You can't marry Elvis, and he's
not a minister, so he can't
marry you, but he can renew
your vows. In the basic $199
package, the King walks you
down the aisle and sings two
songs; pay $799 and you get
two "duelling Elvises", young
and old.

The rest of the city

A glance at any map will tell you that there's a lot more to Las Vegas than simply downtown and the Strip; well over a million people live in the valley as a whole. This is not a city where under-explored neighbourhoods hold fascinating and little-known attractions, however. It's a vast and overwhelmingly residential sprawl that you'll need a car and plenty of time to explore at all thoroughly. Even then, almost all you'll find will be casinos, malls, bars and restaurants; this chapter highlights the pick of the bunch. In addition to the few that genuinely compete with the best of the Strip – the Hard Rock Hotel, the Palms and the Rio – it focuses on the so-called "locals casinos" throughout the city. While these can't match the wow factor of the Strip giants, they find their own niche by offering good-value food, drink and entertainment.

DIG THIS!

3012 S Rancho Drive ☎ 702 222 4344, ⓦ www.digthisvegas.com. Daily 8am–5pm; advance reservations essential. Big Dig $249, Mega Dig $449. MAP P.95, POCKET MAP A11

Las Vegas has always specialized in making adult fantasies come true, but it took a truly inspired entrepreneur to come up with the idea for **Dig This!** On a patch of desert waste ground, a mile west of the Strip, customers get to operate their very own piece of heavy machinery. On payment of a substantial fee, anyone aged 14 and over can drive either a bulldozer or an excavator for ninety minutes; that's a Big Dig, while a Mega Dig lets you do both. Not only do you not need a driving licence, you don't even need to be old enough to have one.

After a few minutes' training you're allowed to sit alone in your vehicle, linked via headphones to an instructor who has an override switch. In a bulldozer, you pile up a huge mound of sand and then power

HARD ROCK HOTEL

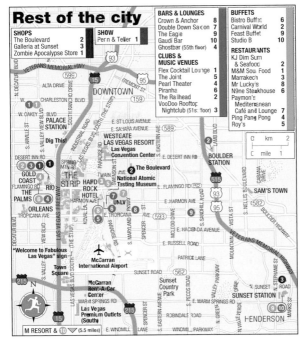

Rest of the city

SHOPS
The Boulevard 2
Galleria at Sunset 3
Zombie Apocalypse Store 1

SHOW
Penn & Teller 1

BARS & LOUNGES
Crown & Anchor 8
Double Down Saloon 7
The Eagle 9
Gaudí Bar 10
Ghostbar (55th floor) 4

CLUBS & MUSIC VENUES
Flex Cocktail Lounge 1
The Joint 5
Pearl Theater 4
Piranha 6
The Railhead 2
VooDoo Rooftop Nightclub (51st floor) 3

BUFFETS
Bistro Buffet 6
Carnival World 2
Feast Buffet 9
Studio B 10

RESTAURANTS
KJ Dim Sum & Seafood 2
M&M Soul Food 1
Marrakech 3
Mr Lucky's 8
N9ne Steakhouse 6
Paymon's Mediterranean Café and Lounge 7
Ping Pang Pong 4
Roy's 5

---

the dozer over the top; in an excavator, you dig trenches and play "basketball" using your scoop. The point, of course, is that it's all fantastic fun. Whether they do it as a retirement treat or a hen party escapade, everyone who has a go seems to come away exhilarated.

GOLD COAST

4000 W Flamingo Rd ☎ 702 367 7111, ⓦ www .goldcoastcasino.com. MAP ABOVE, POCKET MAP G15
One of Las Vegas's first "locals casinos", targeted at city residents themselves, the **Gold Coast** was erected half a mile west of the Strip in 1986. While it swiftly acquired much fancier neighbours, in the shape of the Rio and the Palms, it's hung on to its rather staid Western decor, and remains geared towards a local crowd, especially from the city's Chinatown immediately to the

north. As well as some good Asian restaurants, it also holds a seventy-lane bowling alley.

HARD ROCK HOTEL

4455 Paradise Rd ☎ 702 693 5000, ⓦ www .hardrockhotel.com. MAP ABOVE, POCKET MAP B16
Flagged by two enormous guitars, the **Hard Rock Hotel** clamours for attention a mile east of the Strip. Best seen as a self-sufficient party resort, it fills every weekend with southern Californians who come to soak up the rock'n'roll atmosphere of its clubs, music venues and "daylife"-oriented pool. For sightseers there's little here apart from endless display cabinets of stage clothes and instruments, from Elvis to Bruce and beyond. Spend a night or two, though (ideally to coincide with a big gig), and enjoy its excellent bars and restaurants, and you might just have the time of your life.

M RESORT

12300 Las Vegas Blvd S, Henderson
☎ 702 797 1000, ⓦ themresort.com. MAP P.95

Surveying the city from its
hillside perch near the southern
end of the Las Vegas Valley, ten
miles south of Mandalay Bay,
the shiny **M Resort** opened in
2009. Sadly, the economic
climate was far from ideal for
the smartest new off-Strip casino
to be built in many years, so
despite its impressive contemporary architecture and
well-considered amenities it was
soon struggling. Within two
years, it was snapped up by Penn
Gaming for barely a quarter of
its original billion-dollar cost.

Through it all, the M is
looking as good as ever – almost
in the Wynn class. With lavish
public spaces including a lovely
Palm Springs-style pool complex
and great restaurants like the
hugely popular *Studio B* buffet
and irresistible *Baby Cakes*
bakery, it's unusual in appealing
to locals and visitors alike.

NATIONAL ATOMIC TESTING MUSEUM

755 E Flamingo Rd ☎ 702 794 5151,
ⓦ nationalatomictestingmuseum.org.
Mon–Sat 10am–5pm, Sun noon–5pm. $22;
senior citizens, students and ages 7–17 $20;
under-6s free. MAP P.95, POCKET MAP B12

Between 1951 and 1958, a
remote desert area sixty miles
northwest of Las Vegas,
designated as the Nevada Test
Site, was used for above-ground
tests of atomic bombs.
Mushroom clouds were visible
from the city and tourists
would time their holidays so
they could watch the blasts.
That astonishing saga is
explored in the **National
Atomic Testing Museum**,
which covers not only the
political, scientific and military
background, but also the
kitschy ways in which popular

culture celebrated the bomb.
A separate **Area 51** exhibit
examines the even more
unbelievable story of supposed
"alien autopsies" in the same
general vicinity.

ORLEANS

4500 W Tropicana Ave ☎ 702 365 7111,
ⓦ www.orleanscasino.com. MAP P.95,
POCKET MAP A12

Owned by the same manage-
ment as the Gold Coast (see
p.95), to which it's linked by
free shuttles, the **Orleans** is
roughly a mile due west of New
York–New York. Several of its
restaurants and bars play on
the New Orleans connection
suggested by its name, but
really the emphasis is on
catering to more local tastes,
via such means as an
eighteen-screen cinema and
24-hour bowling alley. As a
place to gamble at above-
average odds and then relax
over cheap food and entertainment, it's hard to beat.

THE PALMS

4321 W Flamingo Rd ☎ 702 942 7777,
ⓦ palms.com. MAP P.95, POCKET MAP F16

It's a cruel drawback of running
a relatively small off-Strip

casino that as soon as you come up with brilliant ideas to lure visitors, the big boys simply copy your innovations and entice your customers back. When it opened across from the Rio in 2001, the **Palms** became the first Las Vegas casino to tap into the twenty-first century's mix of street and celebrity culture, with an array of youth-oriented clubs and theatres that made it the hippest hangout in the city. Since then, the Strip giants have added their own state-of-the-art nightclubs and the Palms has had to keep upping its game.

Despite recent money worries, the basic elements of the Palms' winning formula remain pretty much intact. Nightlife options including the penthouse *Moon* club and the *Ghostbar* alongside it still draw in the crowds, while the Pearl Theater ranks among the city's premier concert venues. The Palms even holds a world-class recording studio as well, used by artists from Lady Gaga and Katy Perry to Usher and Tony Bennett. And with its own cinema, some decent budget restaurants and a good-value buffet, it's careful not to neglect locals either.

RIO

3700 W Flamingo Rd ☎ 866 746 7671, ⓦ www.caesars.com/rio-las-vegas. MAP P.95, POCKET MAP H5

A proud purple beacon, half a mile west of Caesars Palace across the interstate, when it opened in 1990, the **Rio** looked as though it might become the first casino in a generation to threaten the Strip's domination. It was independently owned and played on its Rio de Janeiro theme to build a reputation as the city's premier party scene for locals and visitors alike. Then, as now, all its guest rooms were sizeable suites, sold at highly competitive rates.

In 1999, however, the Rio was sold for almost a billion dollars to what later became Caesars Entertainment. Now run as an adjunct to its sister properties on the central Strip – to which it's linked by free shuttle buses (daily 10am–1am) from Harrah's (see p.61) and Bally's (see p.57) – it can therefore seem like something of an afterthought.

Every June and July, the Rio hosts the high-profile **World Series of Poker**; Caesars acquired the rights to the tournament when it purchased its previous home, Binion's Horseshoe, in 2004. For the rest of the year, it's best known for its sky-high *VooDoo Rooftop Nightclub* (see p.103) the Penn and Teller magic show (see p.103) and its fine selection of restaurants and buffets.

The Rio is also home to the **VooDoo Zipline** ($27.50; daily 11am–11pm), a thrill ride that connects the rooftops of its two towers, nearly 500ft above ground level. Participants are strapped into exposed side-by-side seats, and the experience resembles riding in the scariest ski lift you ever saw.

SAM'S TOWN

5111 Boulder Hwy ☎ 702 456 7777, ⓦ www
.samstownlv.com. MAP P.95, POCKET MAP D12

Best known these days as the
name of an album by Las
Vegas's favourite home-grown
band, the Killers, **Sam's Town** is
a locals casino that stands six
miles east of the Strip, alongside
the main road out to the Hoover
Dam. While maintaining its
long-standing Wild West image,
it has flirted in recent years
with new affiliations such as
NASCAR racing, hosting the
now-defunct Sam's Town 300
race. It has also roofed over
its central courtyard, adding
gardens and waterfalls to create
Mystic Falls Park, the scene of
regular sound-and-light shows
(daily 2pm, 6pm, 8pm & 10pm).

SUNSET STATION

1301 W Sunset Rd, Henderson ☎ 702 547
7777, ⓦ sunsetstation.sclv.com. MAP P.95,
POCKET MAP D13

The self-styled "Spanish
Mediterranean" **Sunset Station**
casino was the first major casino
to be built in the fast-growing
suburb of Henderson, eight
miles southeast of the Strip. It
opened in 1997 as the flagship
property of the so-called

"Stations chain" of locals casinos,
and while the chain as a whole
has experienced financial
uncertainties in recent years,
Sunset Station itself is still
looking good.

Its primary customers being
drawn from its own neighbourhood, Sunset Station is
crammed with community
assets like the huge 72-lane,
24-hour StrikeZone bowling
alley, a 13-screen cinema, and,
rather more questionably, the
Kids Quest daycare centre
that'll look after children while
their parents are gambling.
Some of its features would be
impressive even on the Strip,
however, including the amazing
undulating *Gaudí Bar* (see
p.102), which is the centrepiece
of the casino floor.

WESTGATE LAS VEGAS RESORT

3000 Paradise Rd ☎ 702 732 5111,
ⓦ westgateresorts.com. MAP P.95, POCKET MAP L5

The **Westgate Las Vegas Resort**
used to be the largest and most
famous hotel in the world. Built
by legendary entrepreneur
Kirk Kerkorian in 1969, half a
mile east of the Strip, it was
originally the International
Hotel. Renamed the Las Vegas
Hilton four years later, it
earned its place in history by
hosting Elvis Presley for 837
sell-out concerts, starting with
his comeback appearance in
July 1969 and continuing until
his final Las Vegas appearance
in December 1976. A bronze
statue now commemorates the
King's achievements. Neither
having its own Monorail
station nor standing next to the
city's Convention Center spared
it a battering by the current
recession, however, and in 2012
it went into foreclosure and lost
the Hilton name. Its restaurants
and music venues are still just
about ticking along, but it feels
very peripheral indeed.

SUNSET STATION

Shops

THE BOULEVARD

3528 S Maryland Parkway ☎ 702 732 8949,
🖰 boulevardmall.com. Mon–Sat 10am–9pm,
Sun 11am–7pm. MAP P.95, POCKET MAP B12
A landmark for local shoppers
since 1966 – long before
anyone dreamed of opening
stores on the Strip – the
Boulevard mall is still going
strong. Anchored by the likes
of Macy's and JC Penney, it's
a handy stop-off for day-to-
day shopping.

GALLERIA AT SUNSET

1300 W Sunset Rd, Henderson ☎ 702 434
0202, 🖰 www.galleriaatsunset.com. Mon–Sat
10am–9pm, Sun 11am–6pm. MAP P.95,
POCKET MAP D13
Massive suburban shopping
mall across from Sunset
Station, eight miles southeast of
the Strip, with five department
stores and a host of middle-
American chains.

ZOMBIE APOCALYPSE STORE

3420 Spring Mountain Rd ☎ 866 784 7882,
🖰 zombiestore.biz. Daily: summer 10am–9pm,
winter 10am–7pm. MAP P.95, POCKET MAP A12
Everything you'll need to cope
with the impending zombie
apocalypse, from emergency
rations to knives and swords.
You can also sign up to spend an
evening shooting "real zombies",
with real paintball guns.

Buffets

BISTRO BUFFET

The Palms, 4321 W Flamingo Rd ☎ 702 953
7679, 🖰 palms.com. Breakfast Mon–Sat
8–11am $10; brunch Sun 8am–4pm $22;
lunch Mon–Sat 11am–4pm $14; dinner daily
4–9pm $21. MAP P.95, POCKET MAP F16
A bright, modern space
adjoining the main casino floor,
the Palms' buffet is popular
with locals for its ease of access
and range of world cuisines; be
sure to sample the succulent
ham hocks.

CARNIVAL WORLD

Rio, 3700 W Flamingo Rd ☎ 702 777 7777,
🖰 www.caesars.com/rio-las-vegas. Breakfast
Mon–Fri 8–11am $17; Sat & Sun 8–10am
$17; lunch Mon–Fri 11am–3pm $25;
champagne brunch Sat & Sun 8am–3pm $32;
dinner daily 3–10pm $33, or $48 seafood.
MAP P.95, POCKET MAP H15
Crowds flock to the Rio's
buffet to pile their plates with
everything from sushi to
corndogs; the choice is endless,
even if the quality is only
exceptional in the evening's
sumptuous seafood spread.

FEAST BUFFET

Sunset Station, 1301 W Sunset Rd
☎ 702 547 7777, 🖰 sunsetstation.sclv.com.
Breakfast Mon–Sat 8–11am $9; brunch Sun
8am–4pm $15; lunch Mon–Sat 11am–4pm
$11; dinner daily 4–9pm $15 MAP P.95,
POCKET MAP D13
Unlike their Strip rivals, all
the Stations casinos still offer
cut-price buffets to lure Las
Vegans out to eat and gamble.
Sunset Station has the nicest
dining room; pick carefully and
you can get a great-value meal
including dishes like Indian
curries, seldom seen elsewhere.

STUDIO B

M Resort, 12300 Las Vegas Blvd S ☎ 702 797 1000, ⓦ themresort.com. Lunch Mon–Thurs 11am–2.30pm $17; brunch Fri 11am–2pm $25, Sat & Sun 11am–8.30pm $40; dinner Mon–Thurs 2.30–8.30pm $24, Fri 2.30–8.30pm $40. MAP P.95

Primarily this is a buffet, with food (and prices) to match the very best on the Strip, but it's also a "studio" because chefs demonstrate their art here on stage and TV screens. Prices include free wine and beer; the higher evening and weekend rates cover seafood spreads that include raw oysters. Allow time to get here – it's ten miles south of the Strip – and expect to queue to get in.

Restaurants

KJ DIM SUM & SEAFOOD

Rio, 3700 W Flamingo Rd ☎ 702 777 7777, ⓦ www.caesars.com/rio-las-vegas. Daily 10am–2am. MAP P.95, POCKET MAP H15

This offshoot of a popular restaurant in Las Vegas's nearby Chinatown has been an instant hit, especially for lunching locals who come to select succulent $3–6 dumplings and seafood specialities from the gleaming dim sum trolleys.

KJ DIM SUM & SEAFOOD

Later on, full-sized mains like sizzling scallops or whole steamed fish cost $20–30.

M&M SOUL FOOD

3923 W Charleston Blvd ☎ 702 453 7685, ⓦ mmsoulfoodcafe.com. Daily 7am–8pm. MAP P.95, POCKET MAP A11

Genuine soul food being hard to come by in Las Vegas, this neighbourhood diner is a godsend. Four miles west of downtown, it's best reached by car; you won't be in a fit state to walk anywhere once you've filled up on a $14 plate of their succulent chicken, ribs, gumbo or cornbread.

MARRAKECH

3900 Paradise Rd ☎ 702 737 5611, ⓦ marrakechvegas.com. Daily 5.30–11pm. MAP P.95, POCKET MAP B12

All-you-can-eat banquets of rich, tasty Moroccan food, costing $50 per person and eaten with your fingers from low-lying tables where you sit on scattered cushions. Meaty couscous and pastry dishes are complemented by seafood alternatives, and followed by heavy desserts. Come to enjoy the Middle Eastern atmosphere, belly dancers and all; this is not a place for a quick meal on your own.

MR LUCKY'S

Hard Rock Hotel, 4455 Paradise Rd ☎ 702 693 5592, ⓦ www.hardrockhotel.com. Daily 24hr. MAP P.95, POCKET MAP A16

A refreshing modern take on the traditional Las Vegas all-night casino coffee shop, with an open kitchen and stylish patio seating. Whether you grab a prime rib French dip sandwich for lunch ($16) or stumble in for 4am spaghetti and meatballs (also $16), *Mr Lucky's* offers a round-the-clock break from the Hard Rock frenzy.

N9NE STEAKHOUSE

Palms, 4321 W Flamingo Rd ☎ 702 933
9900, ⓦ www.palms.com. Mon–Thurs & Sun
5.30–10pm, Fri & Sat 5.30–11pm. MAP P.95,
POCKET MAP F16

With its waterfalls, constant
play of lights and glass-walled
celebrity areas, this glitzy,
high-concept restaurant is very
much a place to see and be
seen, but its beautifully
presented resort cuisine, which
includes sushi and sashimi as
well as steak, cannot be faulted.
You can pay well over $50 for
a steak, but the weekday
Happy Hour menu (Mon–Fri
5.30–7.30pm) is great value.

PAYMON'S MEDITERRANEAN CAFÉ AND LOUNGE

4147 S Maryland Parkway at Flamingo Rd
☎ 702 731 6030, ⓦ paymons.com. Daily
11am–1am. MAP P.95, POCKET MAP B12

A truly local restaurant, busy
until late with students from
the nearby university. While
not exclusively vegetarian –
meat-eaters can enjoy dishes
like the $14 Persian chicken-
and-walnut *fesenjan* – it's
especially recommended for
its extensive array of Middle
Eastern classics such as falafel,
hummus and *baba ghanoush*,
available singly or in a $15
combination platter.

PING PANG PONG

Gold Coast, 4000 W Flamingo Rd ☎ 702
367 7111, ⓦ www.goldcoastcasino.com.
Daily 10am–3pm & 5pm–3am. MAP P.95,
POCKET MAP F15

You can tell straight away that
this is the best Chinese
restaurant in any Las Vegas
casino; most of the diners are
Chinese and the menu is
written in Chinese characters
as well as English. Dim sum
makes a lunchtime treat, while
later on you can get chicken
noodles for just $10 or half a
roast duck for $16.

ROY'S

ROY'S

620 E Flamingo Rd ☎ 702 691 2053,
ⓦ roysrestaurant.com. Mon–Thurs
5.30–9.30pm, Fri 5.30–10pm, Sat 5–10pm,
Sun 5–9.30pm. MAP P.95, POCKET MAP B12

Generally considered the best
non-casino restaurant in Las
Vegas, Hawaiian chef Roy
Yamaguchi's dazzling,
dinner-only Pacific Rim
showcase serves exquisite
Asian-influenced cuisine. Mains
like beef short ribs or *misoyaki*
butterfish cost around $30 on
average, but there's usually a
three-course $39 set menu.

Bars and lounges

CROWN & ANCHOR

1350 E Tropicana Ave ☎ 702 739 8676,
ⓦ crownandanchorlv.com. Daily 24hr. MAP P.95,
POCKET MAP B12

The closest Las Vegas comes
to having a genuine British
pub – complete with Cornish
pasties, ploughman's lunches
and Sunday roasts – although
most of its customers, even
when it's showing European
soccer (or rather, football)
games, are students from the
nearby university.

DOUBLE DOWN SALOON

4640 Paradise Rd ☎ 702 791 5775,
Ⓦ doubledownsaloon.com. Daily 24hr.
MAP P.95, POCKET MAP C17

Archetypal hole-in-the-wall
dive bar, situated one block
south of the Hard Rock. The
interior features funky murals
and a hard-edged punk
jukebox. There are no-cover
live bands most nights, plus
slots, blackjack and pool, and
signature drinks like "ass juice"
and bacon martinis.

THE EAGLE

3430 E Tropicana Ave ☎ 702 458 8662, no
website. Daily 24hr. MAP P.95, POCKET MAP C12

This veteran of Las Vegas's gay
scene, located four miles east
of the Strip, has seen its glitzier
rivals come and go, but the
regulars still flock in for
long-standing nights like the
Tues & Fri underwear parties.

GAUDÍ BAR

Sunset Station, 1301 W Sunset Rd,
Henderson ☎ 702 547 7777, Ⓦ sunsetstation
.sclv.com. Daily 24hr. MAP P.95, POCKET MAP D13

The coolest bar in any Las Vegas
casino, created in honour of
Catalan architect Antoni Gaudí,
this bizarre fungoid excrescence
undulates through the heart of

Sunset Station, with cracked-up
mosaics across its cave-like
walls and light courtesy of the
colourful stained-glass panels in
the ceiling.

GHOSTBAR

Palms, 4321 W Flamingo Rd ☎ 702 942
6832, Ⓦ www.palms.com. Daily 8pm–dawn.
Cover Mon–Thurs & Sun $10, Fri & Sat $20.
MAP P.95, POCKET MAP F16

What do you call a club with
DJs and a cover charge but
no dancing? It must be an
ultra-lounge – and there's no
better place to appreciate Las
Vegas at night than from the
deck of this 55th-floor bar,
where the glass floor is replaced
every two weeks.

Clubs and music venues

FLEX COCKTAIL LOUNGE

4371 W Charleston Blvd ☎ 702 385 3539,
Ⓦ flexlasvegas.com. Daily 24hr. No cover.
MAP P.95, POCKET MAP A11

Lively gay bar and club, with
pool tables, slots and an
emphasis on upbeat action.
Free entertainment nightly,
including late-night drag shows
Thursday and Saturday, plus
half-price Happy Hours 4–7pm
and 4–7am.

THE JOINT

Hard Rock Hotel, 4455 Paradise Rd
☎ 702 693 5222, Ⓦ www.hardrockhotel.com.
See website for schedule and prices. MAP P.95,
POCKET MAP B16

Totally revamped in 2009, the
Hard Rock's theatre attracts
four-thousand-strong crowds
to see big-name touring acts.
In addition, groups like
Guns'n'Roses take up residence
for a month or more at a time,
with typical ticket prices of
around $100.

DOUBLE DOWN SALOON

GAUDI BAR

PEARL THEATER

Palms, 4321 W Flamingo Rd ☎ 702 944 3200, ⓦ www.palms.com. See website for current schedule and prices. MAP P.95, POCKET MAP F16

The Palms' state-of-the-art theatre may be smaller than the Hard Rock's Joint, but with its great sound and atmosphere it attracts its fair share of major-league acts across the spectrum, from hip-hop and R&B to reggae and rock.

PIRANHA

4633 Paradise Rd ☎ 702 791 0100, ⓦ piranhavegas.com. Daily 10pm–5am. Cover varies, typically $20. MAP P.95, POCKET MAP B17

The jewel of the so-called "Fruit Loop" and the pulsating heart of Las Vegas's gay nightlife, the spectacular *Piranha* club is approached via either a fiery waterfall or a piranha-filled aquarium. The similarly lavish *8½ Ultra-lounge* alongside makes a perfect spot to kick off the night.

THE RAILHEAD

Boulder Station, 4111 Boulder Hwy ☎ 702 432 7777, ⓦ boulderstation.sclv.com. Daily 24hr. Concert tickets typically $15–40. MAP P.95, POCKET MAP C11

A run-of-the-mill member of the Stations chain of locals casinos, Boulder Station's one bright spot is this large lounge/theatre, which hosts Latin nights on Fridays and Sundays, but also puts on solid mid-range country, soul and blues acts.

VOODOO ROOFTOP NIGHTCLUB

Rio, 3700 W Flamingo Rd ☎ 702 777 6875, ⓦ www.caesars.com/rio-las-vegas. Mon–Thurs & Sun 8pm–2am, Fri & Sat 8pm–3am. Cover $20 and up. MAP P.95, POCKET MAP J15

Long famed for its stunning 51st-floor views, this New Orleans-tinged rendezvous made its reputation as an ultra-hip drinking spot. Now a fully fledged nightclub, it's smaller than its newer rivals on the Strip, but the location is as good as ever and offers a great night out at more affordable prices.

Show

PENN & TELLER

Rio, 3700 W Flamingo Rd ☎ 702 777 2782, ⓦ pennandteller.com. Mon–Wed, Sat & Sun 9pm. $77–93. MAP P.95, POCKET MAP H15

Magicians Penn (the talkative one) and Teller (the other one) have been performing at the Rio since 2000 – while still keeping up their TV careers – but the show remains fresh, whether you simply want to swoon at the magic or you love the behind-the-scenes tricks-of-the-trade patter. They're also great with their audiences, posing and signing happily for groups of fans after the show.

The deserts

Las Vegas stands close to some of the most extraordinary landscapes on the planet – the stark, sublime deserts of the American Southwest. It's possible to get a taste of this red-rock wonderland on brief forays from the city, either to Red Rock Canyon, Hoover Dam and Lake Mead, or to the Valley of Fire. To appreciate its full splendour, however, you need to venture further afield. The primary goal for many visitors is the Grand Canyon, though you'd do better to visit the canyon's South Rim, almost three hundred miles east, than Grand Canyon West, which is closer to hand. Utah's Zion Canyon arguably makes an even better destination for an overnight trip from Las Vegas.

RED ROCK CANYON

17 miles west of the Strip ☎ 702 515 5367, ⓦ www.redrockcanyonlv.org. Visitor centre daily 8am–4.30pm. Scenic Drive daily: March & Oct 6am–7pm, April–Sept 6am–8pm, Nov–Feb 6am–5pm. $7/vehicle, $3 for bikes, motorbikes and pedestrians. MAP BELOW.

For a quick blast of dramatic Southwestern scenery and searing desert sun, simply drive west on any road from

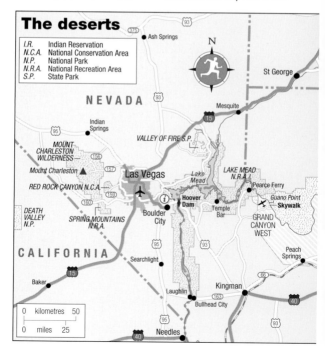

The deserts

I.R.	Indian Reservation
N.C.A.	National Conservation Area
N.P.	National Park
N.R.A.	National Recreation Area
S.P.	State Park

NEVADA

Ash Springs

St George

Mesquite

Indian Springs

VALLEY OF FIRE S.P.

MOUNT CHARLESTON WILDERNESS

Mount Charleston

Las Vegas

Lake Mead

LAKE MEAD N.R.A.

RED ROCK CANYON N.C.A.

Pearce Ferry

Guano Point
Skywalk

DEATH VALLEY N.P.

SPRING MOUNTAINS N.R.A.

Boulder City

Hoover Dam

Temple Bar

GRAND CANYON WEST

CALIFORNIA

Searchlight

Peach Springs

Baker

Laughlin

Bullhead City

Kingman

Needles

0 kilometres 50
0 miles 25

RED ROCK CANYON

the Strip. Tucked behind the first low scrubby hills, the **Red Rock Canyon National Conservation Area** centres on a desert basin at the foot of towering 3000ft cliffs. Ideally, come in the morning when the glowing red rocks are spotlit by the rising sun, and the day's heat has yet to set in fully. Staff at the visitor centre will introduce you to this unforgiving but beautiful wilderness, as well as pointing out the hiking trails and climbing routes that set off from the one-way, thirteen-mile **Scenic Drive** just beyond, which is the only way to see the canyon itself.

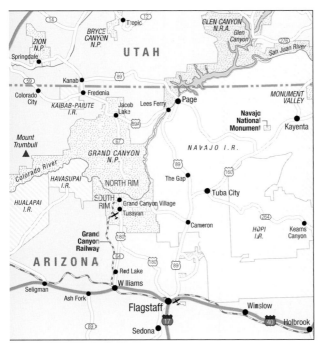

HOOVER DAM

30 miles southeast of the Strip ☎ 702 494 2517, ⓦ www.usbr.gov/lc/hooverdam. Parking daily 8am–6.15pm; $10. Visitor Center daily: April–Sept 9am–6pm; Oct–March 9am–5pm; $10. Powerplant Tour April–Sept 9.25am–4.55pm; Oct–March 9.25am–3.55pm; $15 including Visitor Center, senior citizens & ages 4–16 $12. Dam Tour April–Sept Mon–Thurs 9.30am–4pm, Fri & Sat 9.30am–4.30pm; Oct–March daily 9.30am–3.45pm; all-inclusive fee $30, no reductions, minimum age 8. MAP PP.104–105

The mighty **Hoover Dam** straddles the Colorado River and thus the Nevada–Arizona state line as well. While this graceful 726ft-tall concrete marvel does not, as many visitors imagine, supply a significant proportion of the electricity that keeps Las Vegas running, its construction during the 1930s triggered the growth spurt, and the gambling boom, that created the modern city.

The main highway to Arizona, US-83, crosses the Colorado on a new bridge, slightly downstream from the dam. To see the dam itself, leave the highway via the spur roads at either end. For a quick look you can park briefly on the Arizona side and walk out atop the dam. Otherwise, park in the multistorey garage on the Nevada side, and walk down to the Visitor Center. Displays there explain the story and inner workings of the dam, but paying just a little extra entitles you to join a Power-plant Tour, and ride an elevator down to its base. The hour-long Dam Tour takes you right into its bowels, to explore its dank and mysterious tunnels.

LAKE MEAD

30 miles southeast of the Strip ☎ 702 293 8990, ⓦ www.nps.gov/lake. Visitor Center daily 9am–4.30pm. MAP PP.104–105

Created by the construction of the Hoover Dam, **Lake Mead**, east of Las Vegas, is the largest artificial lake in the USA when full. Its deep blue waters make an extraordinary contrast against the arid sands and red-rock cliffs of the desert, and attract huge numbers of visitors. Only its Nevada shoreline is accessible by road, most easily via Boulder City, a thirty-mile drive from the Strip.

Call in at the **Visitor Center** just off US-93, which has recently been expanded and renovated and holds some fascinating models and exhibits, then follow the **Lakeshore Scenic Drive** down to the lake itself. How close it approaches the shore depends on current water levels, which have

HOOVER DAM

remained low since 2002. Both **Lake Mead Marina** (☎702 293 3484, ⓦwww.riverlakes.com) and the neighbouring **Las Vegas Boat Harbor** (☎702 293 1191, ⓦwww.boatinglakemead .com) rent out boats and jet-skis, while the **Desert Princess** paddle steamer offers lake cruises from the latter ($26–61.50; ☎866 292 9191, ⓦwww.lakemeadcruises.com).

MOUNT CHARLESTON

A real anomaly in the Nevada deserts, and one that tends to be appreciated more by locals than by visitors, the Spring Mountain range soars into the sky forty miles northwest of the Strip. Its highest peak, **Mount Charleston**, stands just under 12,000ft tall, so its forested slopes offer a welcome escape from the summer heat of the city. Several appealing hiking trails set off across the surrounding hillsides.

To reach the mountains, head northwest out of Las Vegas on US-95 then turn west onto Hwy-157, which snakes its way into **Kyle Canyon**. Up at the head of the canyon, the **Mary Jane Falls Trail** is a 2.5-mile round-trip trek that climbs via gruelling switchbacks to a pair of waterfalls. Half a mile further on, the three-mile **Cathedral Rock Trail** involves a demanding thousand-foot ascent to a promontory with onward views to Charleston Peak itself.

That's as far as most people go, but with a little more time you can drive north from Kyle Canyon to **Lee Canyon** along Hwy-158 to enjoy far-reaching views over the desert wasteland where Nevada's notorious A-bomb tests took place in the 1950s, and then return to US-95 via Hwy-56.

VALLEY OF FIRE STATE PARK

VALLEY OF FIRE STATE PARK

Just over 50 miles northeast of the Strip ☎702 397 2088, ⓦvalley-of-fire.com. Visitor centre daily 8.30am–4.30pm. $10/vehicle. MAP PP.104–105

The most mind-blowing red-rock scenery you can see on a driving day-trip lies in the Valley of Fire State Park. To get there, follow I-15 for thirty miles towards Utah, then turn right onto Hwy-169. The park begins just after you cross the ridge of **Muddy Mountain** to look out over a magnificent landscape of incandescent, multicoloured peaks and cliffs stretching all the way to Lake Mead.

A roadside visitor centre explains local history and geology, and displays live rattlesnakes. It marks the start of a five-mile, dead-end road that winds through amazing rock outcrops that can be explored on short hiking trails. The single most extraordinary formation, however, lies a further three miles along Hwy-169, where a natural arch – **Elephant Rock** – looks like a giant elephant poking its trunk into the sands.

Keep driving east, and you can loop back to Las Vegas along the north shore of **Lake Mead** – a total round trip of 130 miles.

Grand Canyon tours

The Grand Canyon is not as near Las Vegas as you might imagine. **Grand Canyon National Park** is two hundred miles east of Las Vegas, and the **South Rim** (see p.109), which holds the park's main tourist facilities and viewpoints, is a drive of almost three hundred miles each way from the city. To see the canyon on a day-trip, there are two options: a long bus ride or an expensive flight. The majority of tours from Las Vegas therefore go to **Grand Canyon West** (see below), more like one hundred miles from the city, which while less spectacular is also home to the **Skywalk**, and offers the chance to land by, and even take a rafting trip on, the **Colorado River**.

With most of the operators listed below, you can choose between taking a **tour** to Grand Canyon West or the South Rim, by bus, helicopter or plane. Bus tours to Grand Canyon West typically cost around $100, or $135 including the Skywalk. The entire round-trip takes at least twelve hours, including four hours at Grand Canyon West itself. A **bus tour** to the South Rim takes over sixteen hours, with less time at the canyon itself. Prices can be as low as $80, but expect to pay more like $150 for a deluxe coach.

Flight-seeing tours to Grand Canyon West start at around $150 by plane (without landing) or $250 by helicopter. Expect to pay at least $250 by plane or $300 by helicopter for a tour that includes walking on the Skywalk, and at least $500 for a helicopter tour that lands down by the river as well.

All **flights** to the South Rim are in fixed-wing planes. A flight with a ground tour of canyon viewpoints by bus will cost around $250. Tours that include a separate helicopter flight once you arrive cost at least $400.

Note that many flights depart not from Las Vegas itself, but from **Boulder City**, thirty miles southeast. If you're hoping for an aerial view of the city into the bargain, check which airport your operator uses.

TOUR OPERATORS

Grand Canyon Airlines 🕿 702 835 8484, Ⓦ www.grandcanyonairlines.com.
Maverick 🕿 702 261 0007, Ⓦ www.maverickhelicopter.com.
Papillon 🕿 702 736 7243, Ⓦ www.papillon.com.
Scenic Airlines 🕿 702 638 3300, Ⓦ www.scenic.com.
Sundance 🕿 702 736 0606, Ⓦ www.sundancehelicopters.com.

GRAND CANYON WEST

125 miles east of Las Vegas Ⓦ www.grandcanyonwest.com. If you drive here yourself you'll still have to join a ground tour, costing a minimum of $47/person, or $72 including the Skywalk. MAP PP.104-105

The spot known as **Grand Canyon West** (or the West Rim) is not actually in Grand Canyon National Park, but on the Hualapai Indian Reservation to the west. Although it can be reached via a 125-mile one-way drive from Las Vegas, road conditions are so poor that almost all visitors fly (see box above).

At this point, close to the western end of the Grand Canyon shortly before the Colorado River spills into Lake Mead, the chasm has dwindled to around two miles wide and lacks the extraordinary sculpted rock formations you may be expecting. Instead

SKYWALK, GRAND CANYON WEST

Grand Canyon West consists of a cluster of viewpoints above drops of up to 4000ft, and looking across to similar cliffs on the far side of the river.

The major attraction is the **Skywalk**, a glass-floored, horseshoe-shaped walkway that juts out over the rim of a side canyon at Eagle Point, close to the airstrip where tours begin. The best view of the canyon itself comes from **Guano Point**, a mile or so north. The Hualapai tribe, who have lived here for over a thousand years, offer various other activities, including dance performances and barbecue cookouts.

GRAND CANYON SOUTH RIM

270 miles east of Las Vegas ☏ 928 638 7888, ⓦ www.nps.gov/grca. Entrance fee $30/ vehicle, valid for seven days. MAP PP.104–105
To see the Grand Canyon in all its glory, you have to visit **Grand Canyon National Park**. This is the area familiar from a million movies and photographs, where the canyon is studded with mighty red-rock buttes and pyramids, and measures a mile deep and eleven miles wide.

Tourist facilities, concentrated around several magnificent viewpoints along the canyon's South Rim, can be reached either by road – a total drive from Las Vegas of 270 miles, via the I-40 interstate that crosses northern Arizona fifty miles south of the canyon – or by air, to Tusayan airport, six miles south of the canyon.

While it's possible to visit the **South Rim** on a day-trip (see box opposite), it makes much more sense to drive yourself and stay at least one night. That will give you the chance to spend some time beside the canyon at sunset and dawn, and to sample the evening atmosphere of the splendid old rim-edge *El Tovar* hotel (see p.121).

HOPI POINT, GRAND CANYON SOUTH RIM

ZION NATIONAL PARK

160 miles northeast of Las Vegas ☎ 435 772 3256, Ⓦ www.nps.gov/zion. Entrance fee $30/vehicle, valid for seven days. MAP PP.104–105

Any Las Vegas visitor hoping to see the stupendous desert scenery of the Southwest at its absolute best would do well to consider making a side trip to **Zion National Park**. Located in southwest Utah, a fast, direct drive of 160 miles northeast up I-15 from Las Vegas, it's every bit as impressive as the Grand Canyon, and offers much greater potential for an active weekend excursion from the city.

Named by nineteenth-century Mormon settlers, and carved by the Virgin River, Zion Canyon stands at the heart of the park. Unlike at the Grand Canyon, which is almost always seen from above, visitors enter by following the river upstream from the south and therefore see it from the verdant valley below. Astonishing sheer red-rock walls soar to either side, many of them topped by crests of paler sandstone that have been given fanciful names like the Court of the Patriarchs and the Great White Throne.

At the northern end of the canyon, visitors can follow the easy, mile-long **Riverside Walk** to the point where the Virgin River enters the valley. In the Zion Narrows beyond, accessible only to hardy hikers happy to wade waist-deep in ice-cold water, the towering canyon walls stand just a few feet apart. Other demanding trails switchback out of the valley to reach the desert uplands high above, and make wonderful day-hikes; the **West Rim Trail**, for example, climbs to a slender rock spur known as Angel's Landing, with a sheer quarter-of-a-mile drop to either side. Not surprisingly, Zion is also a favourite destination with rock climbers; several local operators offer guides.

Although it's possible to drive through the southern portion of the park, and continue east (towards Bryce Canyon) via an amazing 1930s tunnel, the only vehicles allowed into the narrowest part of the canyon are free shuttle buses, which depart from the visitor centre beside the park entrance.

In the canyon itself, the veteran *Zion Lodge* (see p.121) offers accommodation and dining, and the park runs large but very pleasant campgrounds. Otherwise, almost all facilities are in the gateway town of **Springdale**, in a magnificent setting just south of the park.

ZION NARROWS, ZION NATIONAL PARK

Restaurants

Mount Charleston

A CUT ABOVE

Resort on Mount Charleston, 2 Kyle Canyon Rd ☎ 702 872 5500, ⓦ mtcharlestonresort .com. Mon–Thurs & Sun 7am–9pm, Fri & Sat 7am–10pm. MAP PP.104–105

Open for all meals daily – though note the early closing time on weekdays – the light, spacious restaurant at this grand old lodge serves hearty mountain specialities such as warming buffalo and boar stew ($10), plus tasty pizzas, pasta and $30 steaks.

MOUNT CHARLESTON LODGE

5375 Kyle Canyon Rd ☎ 702 872 5408, ⓦ mtcharlestonlodge.com. Daily 8am–9pm. MAP PP.104–105

The obvious place to stop for lunch on a Mount Charleston day-trip, where the road up the mountain reaches its dead end, featuring an outdoor patio that enjoys drop-dead views. The food itself is less enthralling, with pizzas and sandwiches for around $13, burgers a little more and a three-course dinner menu for $24.

Grand Canyon

ARIZONA ROOM

Bright Angel Lodge, Grand Canyon South Rim ☎ 928 638 2631, ⓦ www.grandcanyonlodges .com. Daily: March–Oct 11.30am–3pm & 4.30–10pm; Nov & Dec 4.30–10pm. No reservations. MAP PP.104–105

This good-value restaurant, near the rim but with no views, is the most convenient place to pick up a decent meal on the South Rim. Lunchtime burgers, sandwiches and salads cost $9–13, full dinners more like $18 for chicken and $26 for steak.

EL TOVAR DINING ROOM

El Tovar, Grand Canyon South Rim ☎ 928 638 2631, ext 6432, ⓦ www.grandcanyonlodges .com. Daily 6.30–11am, 11.30am–2pm & 4.30–10pm. MAP PP.104–105

The stately splendours of the timber-built *El Tovar* make an impressive setting for great food. Only the front row of tables enjoy partial views of the canyon, but this grand century-old hotel oozes old-fashioned charm and the waiters are happy to let you linger. Reserve ahead for dinner, when mains like half a duck or veal *jaegerschnitzel* cost around $35; lunch and breakfast are first-come first-served and much cheaper.

Springdale

BIT & SPUR RESTAURANT

1212 Zion Park Blvd, Springdale UT ☎ 435 772 3498, ⓦ bitandspur.com. Daily 5–10pm. MAP PP.104–105

With a cosy saloon-like interior, and a terrace facing Zion's red-rock cliffs, this relaxed but high-quality Mexican/Southwestern restaurant makes a wonderful dinner spot. Chilli-rubbed steak costs $28, barbecued ribs $24 and a *chile relleno* (stuffed chilli) just $14, while the outdoor seating makes an ideal venue for a beer after a long day's hiking.

SPOTTED DOG CAFÉ

Flanigan's Inn, 428 Zion Park Blvd, Springdale UT ☎ 435 772 3244, ⓦ flanigans .com. Daily 7–11am & 5–10pm. MAP PP.104–105

This very reasonably priced restaurant is attached to a motel near the Zion park entrance. In the morning it lays out a decent breakfast buffet, while the dinner menu ranges from a highly recommended $22 lamb shank to meatloaf or pasta at more like $15.

Accommodation

Choosing where to stay is the single biggest decision of any Las Vegas trip. Las Vegas is not like other destinations, where it's the city that you've come to see, and your choice of hotel makes little difference. In Las Vegas, it's the hotels that you've come to see – or rather the stupendously large casino resorts that hold not only the hotels, but also the restaurants, clubs, theatres and attractions, as well as the slot machines and gaming tables.

The fundamental choice is whether or not to stay on the **Strip**, which basically means staying in one of the colossal mega-casinos. Las Vegas is currently home to 24 of the world's 42 largest hotels, most along or very close to the Strip. Between them, they hold over 75,000 rooms, an average of almost 4000 each. All of those rooms are at least the standard of a good chain motel, invariably with en-suite bathrooms and with two queen-sized beds as the norm. Many are much more opulent; the standard rooms at places like Wynn, the Venetian and Bellagio are very plush, while every property offers **suites**.

However luxurious the rooms, the experience of staying in a hotel that has several thousand rooms has its drawbacks, including long **check-in queues** (half an hour is considered normal), a lack of personal service and endless walking to and fro. In, say, Caesars Palace or the MGM Grand, it can easily take twenty minutes to walk from your room out onto the Strip. The result is that most visitors spend their time in either their own hotel or its immediate neighbours.

The obvious alternative is to stay **downtown**, which is smaller and on a more manageable scale, with every hotel within easy walking distance from all the rest. While downtown has more affordable gambling and dining,

however, it has very few shops, shows or clubs, and lacks the jaw-dropping architecture of the Strip. It's also possible to find a room **elsewhere in the city**, either in a so-called locals casino, or in one of the many chain motels scattered around the periphery, but it's not recommended for visitors who want to experience all that makes Las Vegas unique.

As for **room rates**, it's essential to be aware that rooms change in price every night according to the level of demand. A room costing $49 on Wednesday may not still be $49 on Saturday; it might well be $199. As a rule, Friday and Saturday are the most expensive nights, though exact rates also depend on factors such as whether there's a big convention in town; a concert at a specific casino; or even a sports event elsewhere, which gamblers want to bet on in Las Vegas.

The one sure way to find a cheap rate is to visit during the week. Beyond that, it's best to book via the hotel's own website a couple of months or more in advance, or, for weekday stays only, at the very last minute. Trying to make a reservation for the coming weekend, or the weekend after, is asking for trouble.

The **prices** given here are broad guidelines to suggest what you might pay during an ordinary, quiet week, and give some idea of how hotels compare.

Resort fees and taxes

Note that in addition to the room rates shown in this chapter, guests in almost every Las Vegas hotel are also required to pay so-called resort fees, listed here separately. These additional daily fees were introduced on the pretext of covering internet access – even if you don't use it – and generally also include such things as local or even long-distance (at Wynn and Encore) phone calls, use of a fitness centre and a newspaper, but *not* parking.

Hotel rates shown here do not include the additional room tax added to all bills, of twelve percent on the Strip, and thirteen percent downtown.

The Strip

ARIA > 3730 Las Vegas Blvd S ☎ 866 359 7757 or ☎ 702 590 7111, ⓦ aria.com. MAP P.45, POCKET MAP B1. CityCenter's focal resort, *Aria*, is perfect for modernists. There's a sleek contemporary aesthetic, and the classy rooms feature big beds, walk-in showers as well as tubs, and on-screen digital controls for everything from curtains to a/c . Check-in can be slow and somewhat anarchic. **Resort fee $35/day. Mon–Thurs & Sun $203, Fri & Sat $238.**

BALLY'S > 3645 Las Vegas Blvd S ☎ 877 603 4390, ⓦ caesars.com/ballys -las-vegas. MAP P.55, POCKET MAP G7. Staying at Bally's is not an experience anyone gets very excited about – the rooms are spacious but otherwise run of the mill – but it is in a great location to make the most of the Strip. Above all, it's connected to its younger sister Paris next door, so guests get the benefits of staying there at much lower rates. **Resort fee $29/day. Mon–Thurs & Sun $82, Fri & Sat $194.**

BELLAGIO > 3600 Las Vegas Blvd S ☎ 888 987 6667 or ☎ 702 693 7111, ⓦ bellagio.com. MAP P.45, POCKET MAP F7. As Las Vegas is forever outdoing itself, Bellagio is no longer the cream of the crop, but by any normal standards its opulent rooms epitomize luxury, while its location and amenities can't be beaten. The premium rooms overlook the lake and its fountains, but the views from the back, over the pool, are great too. **Resort fee $35/day. Mon–Thurs & Sun $209, Fri & Sat $299.**

CAESARS PALACE > 3570 Las Vegas Blvd S ☎ 866 227 5938, ⓦ caesarspalace.com. MAP P.55, POCKET MAP F6. Fond memories of 1960s excess will always form part of the appeal of Caesars Palace, even if these days comfort tends to win over kitsch. The sheer scale of the place can be overwhelming, but with its top-class dining and shopping, plus a fabulous pool and spa, it still has a real cachet. For serious luxury, pay $50–100 extra to stay in the newer Augustus and Octavius towers, with separate entrances for greater privacy. **Resort fee $32/day. Mon–Thurs & Sun $205, Fri & Sat $261.**

CIRCUS CIRCUS > 2880 Las Vegas Blvd S ☎ 800 634 3450 or ☎ 702 734 0410, ⓦ circuscircus.com. MAP P.70, POCKET MAP K8. Long a favourite with families and budget travellers, Circus Circus is showing its age; with its neighbours dropping like flies it feels like the casino time forgot. If you don't plan to linger and you have a car, its rock-bottom rates may prove irresistible. Pay a little extra to stay in its renovated towers, as opposed to the dingy Manor section. **Resort fee $24/day. Mon–Thurs & Sun $27, Fri & Sat $99.**

THE COSMOPOLITAN > 3708 Las Vegas Blvd S ☎ 702 698 7000, ⓦ www .cosmopolitanlasvegas.com. MAP P.45, POCKET MAP F9. Stylish and contemporary, *The Cosmopolitan* is a great option at the heart of the Strip. The comfortable rooms come with colossal beds; even those that aren't suites have large living areas, while all except the cheapest have Strip-view balconies (a rarity in Las Vegas), and many overlook the Bellagio fountains. There's a spa plus top-quality restaurants and clubs, and the rooms aren't far from the lobby or the garage. **Resort fee $30/day. Mon–Thurs & Sun $200, Fri & Sat $320.**

THE CROMWELL > 3595 Las Vegas Blvd S ☎ 702 777 3777, ⓦ www .caesars.com/cromwell. MAP P.55, POCKET MAP G7. Only in Las Vegas does having 188 rooms make you a "boutique hotel"; the Strip's smallest casino reopened in 2014 as an exclusive and expensive hideaway. Resort fee $32/day. Mon–Thurs & Sun $179, Fri & Sat $279.

ENCORE > 3121 Las Vegas Blvd S ☎ 877 321 9966 or ☎ 702 770 8000, ⓦ wynnlasvegas.com. MAP P.70, POCKET MAP J1. Las Vegas doesn't come any more luxurious than this; Encore truly is fit for a prince (just ask Harry Windsor). The huge, high-tech rooms are more subdued and earth-toned than the lurid reds the casino might lead you to expect, and all are suites, although the beds are screened off from the living areas rather than being separate rooms. Resort fee $35/day. Mon–Thurs & Sun $229, Fri & Sat $339.

EXCALIBUR > 3850 Las Vegas Blvd S ☎ 800 879 1397 or ☎ 702 597 7777, ⓦ excalibur.com. MAP P.32, POCKET MAP B4. Cross the drawbridge, enter the Disneyesque castle, wheel your bag through the casino full of kids, ride the elevator to the top of the tower and amazingly enough, so long as you pay a little extra for one of the renovated "wide-screen" rooms, you've found yourself a nice place to stay. The older rooms are looking very worn, though, and with its endless queues Excalibur itself can feel too big for comfort. Resort fee $29/day. Mon–Thurs & Sun $38, Fri & Sat $123.

THE FLAMINGO > 3555 Las Vegas Blvd S ☎ 888 902 9929 or ☎ 702 733 3111, ⓦ www.caesars.com/flamingo -las-vegas. MAP P.55, POCKET MAP G6. So long as you stay at ground level, *The Flamingo* seems like a great hotel – light, airy and central, it's on a manageable scale, and has an attractive garden and pool, and even live flamingoes. The rooms upstairs are very hit and miss, though, and can be grubby; only consider staying here if you find a truly exceptional rate. Resort fee $29/day. Mon–Thurs & Sun $88, Fri & Sat $132.

HARRAH'S > 3475 Las Vegas Blvd S ☎ 800 214 9110, ⓦ www.caesars .com/harrahs-las-vegas. MAP P.55, POCKET MAP G5. There's nothing to quicken the heart about Harrah's, the middle-of-the-Strip, middle-of-the-road casino that spent a couple of decades catering so assiduously to its long-standing customers that it was able to buy all its fancier neighbours. With that kind of success, they haven't felt constrained to change much. The standard rooms are rather ordinary, though there are some fancier suites. Resort fee $29/day. Mon–Thurs & Sun $65, Fri & Sat $150.

THE LINQ > 3535 Las Vegas Blvd S ☎ 800 634 6441, ⓦ thelinq.com. MAP P. 55, POCKET MAP G5. The former Imperial Palace always ranked among the Strip's cheapest options; now renamed the Linq, it's maintaining that tradition by charging surprisingly low rates for such a central location. Resort fee $29/day. Mon–Thurs & Sun $50, Fri & Sat $150.

LUXOR > 3900 Las Vegas Blvd S ☎ 877 386 4658 or ☎ 702 262 4444, ⓦ luxor .com. MAP P.32, POCKET MAP B6. More than twenty years since this futuristic black-glass pyramid opened, it's sadly feeling its age. It can still be a thrill to stay in one of the original rooms, with their sloping windows, but there's a reason rooms in the newer tower next door cost a little more – they're in much better condition, and also have baths and/or jacuzzis instead of showers. Resort fee $29/day. Mon–Thurs & Sun $57, Fri & Sat $156.

MANDALAY BAY > 3950 Las Vegas Blvd S ☎ 877 632 7800 or ☎ 702 632 7777, ⓦ mandalaybay.com. MAP P.32, POCKET MAP B7. This far south of the central Strip, it makes sense to see Mandalay Bay as a self-contained resort. If you're happy to spend long days by its extravagant pool, and while away your evenings in its fine restaurants, bars, clubs and theatres, then it's well worth considering. The rooms are very comfortable, with both baths and walk-in showers. Resort fee $32/day. Mon–Thurs & Sun $90, Fri & Sat $150.

MGM GRAND > 3799 Las Vegas Blvd S ☎ 877 880 0880 or ☎ 702 891 7777, Ⓦ mgmgrand.com. MAP P.32, POCKET MAP C3. While it may not be the world's largest hotel any more, the MGM Grand feels too big for its own good; once you've queued to check in and walked half a mile to your room, you may not feel up to venturing out to explore. Accommodation has been largely upgraded at the expense of its former character; the dark brown palette could be any convention hotel, anywhere. Resort fee $32/day. Mon–Thurs & Sun $94, Fri & Sat $191.

THE MIRAGE > 3400 Las Vegas Blvd S ☎ 800 374 9000 or ☎ 702 791 7111, Ⓦ mirage.com. MAP P.70, POCKET MAP F4. The casino that gave Vegas a new definition of luxury seems like a fairly modest choice almost thirty years on, in that its rooms are smaller than the norm, and its bathrooms even smaller. They're still more than comfortable, though, with Strip and volcano views, and in a good location with excellent on-site amenities. Resort fee $32/day. Mon–Thurs & Sun $169, Fri & Sat $250.

MONTE CARLO/PARK MGM > 3770 Las Vegas Blvd S ☎ 888 529 4828 or ☎ 702 730 7777, Ⓦ montecarlo .com or Ⓦ parkmgm.com. MAP P.45, POCKET MAP C2. At the time of writing, the long-standing but largely anonymous Monte Carlo was undergoing a major overhaul, and due to be split into two separate hotels – the 2700-room Park MGM and the pricier boutique NoMad. Expect much fancier rooms, more in keeping with the upscale CityCenter vibe. Until then, however, its existing rooms can be great value. Resort fee $30/day. Mon–Thurs & Sun $69, Fri & Sat $199.

NEW YORK–NEW YORK > 3790 Las Vegas Blvd S ☎ 866 815 4365 or ☎ 702 740 6969, Ⓦ newyorknewyork .com. MAP P.32, POCKET MAP C3. Spending a night or two in Las Vegas's own Big Apple makes a more appealing prospect than a stay at most of its larger, less compact neighbours. Whether you opt for a "Park Avenue" or a slightly larger "Madison Avenue" room, the guest rooms are attractive and readily accessible, with some nice Art Deco touches, and the casino itself holds some excellent bars and restaurants. Resort fee $30/day. Mon–Thurs & Sun $81, Fri & Sat $179.

Las Vegas's most luxurious spas

State-of-the-art spas in Las Vegas's top casinos pamper visitors with pools, steam rooms, fitness facilities and massage services. Daily entry normally costs around $30, and massages and other treatments from around $100 per half hour. Often, during busy periods, only guests staying in the relevant casino can use its spa. The following are the very best:

Aria	The Spa	Daily 5am–8pm	☎ 702 590 9600
Bellagio	Spa Bellagio	Daily 6am–8pm	☎ 702 693 7472
Caesars Palace	Qua	Daily 6am–8pm	☎ 866 782 0655
The Cosmopolitan	Sahra	Daily 7am–8pm	☎ 702 698 7171
Encore	Spa	Daily 7am–8pm	☎ 702 770 4772
Golden Nugget	Spa	Daily 6am–8pm	☎ 702 386 8186
Hard Rock	Reliquary	Daily 8am–7pm	☎ 702 693 5520
Mandalay Bay	Spa Mandalay	Daily 6am–8.30pm	☎ 877 632 7300
The Mirage	Spa	Daily 6am–7pm	☎ 702 791 7146
Planet Hollywood	Mandara	Daily 7am–7pm	☎ 702 785 5772
The Venetian	Canyon Ranch	Daily 6am–8pm	☎ 702 414 3600
Wynn	Spa	Daily 7am–8pm	☎ 702 770 3900

THE PALAZZO > 3325 Las Vegas Blvd S ☎ 866 263 3001 or ☎ 702 607 7777, ⓦ www.palazzo.com. MAP P.70, POCKET MAP H3. Staying at the Palazzo is fundamentally the same as staying at the Venetian (once you go downstairs, you're in the same building), but you'll find yourself slightly further from the heart of the action here. The actual rooms are very similar, with plush sleeping and living areas at slightly different levels, and huge marble bathrooms. **Resort fee $39/day. Mon–Thurs & Sun $229, Fri & Sat $299.**

PARIS > 3655 Las Vegas Blvd S ☎ 877 796 2096, ⓦ parislasvegas.com. MAP P.55, POCKET MAP G8. For many visitors, Paris represents an ideal compromise – you get to stay in an interesting big-name property, with excellent amenities plus "only in Vegas" features like the Eiffel Tower outside your window – without paying premium prices for opulent fittings you don't really need. The standard rooms are slightly faded now; for a little more pampering, opt for a newer "Red Room". **Resort fee $32/day. Mon–Thurs & Sun $119, Fri & Sat $195.**

PLANET HOLLYWOOD > 3667 Las Vegas Blvd S ☎ 866 919 7472, ⓦ planethollywoodresort.com. MAP P.55, POCKET MAP G9. While Planet Hollywood's confusing layout can make it a long trek from your car to your room, once you're here it's a great-value central location. The rooms are in a style they call "Hollywood Hip", which tends to mean black and gold carpets and wallpaper; movie stills on the wall; and walk-in showers as well as baths. **Resort fee $32/day. Mon–Thurs & Sun $90, Fri & Sat $258.**

SLS LAS VEGAS > 2535 Las Vegas Blvd S ☎ 702 761 7757, ⓦ slslasvegas .com. MAP P.70, POCKET MAP L4. Despite standing well north of the Strip proper, the former Sahara is thriving enough to charge substantial rates for its nicely refurbished rooms. **Resort fee $30/day. Mon–Thurs & Sun $111, Fri & Sat $211.**

THE STRATOSPHERE > 2000 Las Vegas Blvd S ☎ 702 380 7777, ⓦ stratospherehotel.com. MAP P.70, POCKET MAP L2. Much too far to walk

to from either the Strip or downtown, the Stratosphere is at least something of a destination in its own right – the rooms aren't in the 1000ft tower, but guests do get free admission. Find the right cut-price offer online, and its simple but sizeable rooms may suit your budget. **Resort fee $25/day. Mon–Thurs & Sun $46, Fri & Sat $155.**

TI (TREASURE ISLAND) > 3300 Las Vegas Blvd S ☎ 800 944 7444 or ☎ 702 894 7111, ⓦ treasureisland.com. MAP P.70, POCKET MAP G3. Like the building itself, the rooms at TI remain in good condition – they're nothing fancy, but they look reasonably fresh and have good beds – and the location is great too. These days, the whole place, and the pool in particular, attracts a young party crowd. Look out for online discounts. **Resort fee $32/day. Mon–Thurs & Sun $129, Fri & Sat $140.**

THE TROPICANA > 3801 Las Vegas Blvd S ☎ 888 381 8767 or ☎ 702 739 2222, ⓦ www.troplv.com. MAP P.32, POCKET MAP C4. Completely overhauled in 2010, this long-standing landmark can't quite match its Mirage-owned neighbours for dining and nightlife, but is a solid choice for a place to stay. It offers large, cream-and-orange-rooms with new furnishings, an excellent pool complex and a location handy for the airport. **Resort fee $29/day. Mon–Thurs & Sun $119, Fri & Sat $159**

VDARA > 2600 W Harmon Ave ☎ 866 745 7767 or ☎ 702 590 2767, ⓦ vdara.com. MAP P.45, POCKET MAP E9. Hedonist holidaymakers might feel ill at ease with the austere steel-and-chrome aesthetic of this CityCenter all-suite hotel, and its lack of a casino, but if you're here to work, or just fancy an escape from Las Vegas's round-the-clock scene, it makes a peaceful and very comfortable retreat. **Resort fee $35/day. Mon–Thurs & Sun $119, Fri & Sat $199.**

THE VENETIAN > 3355 Las Vegas Blvd S ☎ 866 659 9643 or ☎ 702 414 1000, ⓦ www.venetian.com. MAP P.70, POCKET MAP G4. In terms of amenities in the property as a whole, and sheer comfort in its guest rooms, the Venetian ranks in the very top tier of Strip hotels; slightly more old-fashioned than Wynn, but still a true pampering experience. All the rooms are suites; you step down from the sleeping area, with its huge bed, to reach a sunken living space near the panoramic windows. Unusually, the price for advance bookings often remains the same for weekends as for weekdays. Resort fee $39/day. Mon–Thurs & Sun $229, Fri & Sat $299.

WYNN LAS VEGAS > 3131 Las Vegas Blvd S ☎ 877 321 9966 or ☎ 702 770 7000, Ⓦ wynnlasvegas.com. MAP P.70, POCKET MAP J2. With the arguable exception of the all-but-identical Encore alongside, this is as opulent as it gets in Vegas. The super-large rooms are tastefully decorated and equipped with luxurious linens, and bathrooms feature marble tubs, walk-in showers and even TVs. Resort fee $35/day. Mon–Thurs & Sun $186, Fri & Sat $339.

Downtown

THE D > 301 E Fremont St ☎ 702 388 2400, Ⓦ www.thed.com. MAP P.87, POCKET MAP G12. Since turning from Fitzgerald's into The D, this central downtown hotel has become a real bargain. All its rooms have had a top-to-bottom makeover (each has two queen beds) and the amenities downstairs are much improved. The one problem can be noise from the Experience outside. Resort fee $20/day. Mon–Thurs & Sun $29, Fri & Sat $99.

EL CORTEZ > 600 E Fremont St ☎ 800 634 6703 or ☎ 702 385 5200, Ⓦ elcortezhotelcasino.com. MAP P.87, POCKET MAP H12. Long renowned as Las Vegas's cheapest casino, El Cortez stands a short but, at night, potentially intimidating walk from the heart of Fremont Street. Once there, everything's in good shape, though the "Vintage" rooms, reached via the stairs, are no better than faded motel rooms. The "Cabana" suites, across the street, are much more appealing. Online packages for first-time guests offset room rates

with free meals and gaming. Resort fee $11/day. Mon–Thurs & Sun $28, Fri & Sat $89.

FOUR QUEENS > 202 E Fremont St ☎ 800 634 6045 or ☎ 702 385 4011, Ⓦ www.fourqueens.com. MAP P.87, POCKET MAP G12. There's no real reason to pick this resolutely old-school downtown stalwart over any of its neighbours, though it has at least kept its rooms up to the adequate but unexciting level, say, of a $60-per-night national chain. No resort fee. Mon–Thurs & Sun $39, Fri & Sat $109.

FREMONT HOTEL > 200 E Fremont St ☎ 800 634 6182 or ☎ 702 385 3232, Ⓦ www.fremontcasino.com. MAP P.87, POCKET MAP G12. As one of the few downtown casinos owned by a major corporation – Boyd Gaming – the Fremont keeps its standards pretty high. The rooms are small but up to date, with pleasant decor and linens, and it's really not a bad alternative if you fancy being in the thick of the Fremont Street action. No resort fee. Mon–Thurs & Sun $40, Fri & Sat $140.

THE GOLDEN GATE > 1 E Fremont St ☎ 800 426 1906 or ☎ 702 385 1906, Ⓦ goldengatecasino.com. MAP P.87, POCKET MAP G11. Las Vegas's first ever hotel, one hundred years old in 2006, has been restyled as a 106-room "boutique hotel", with the promise that more suites will soon be added in a new extension. Yes, the rooms are small and the floors strangely lumpy, but you do get a true taste of Vegas history – plus, unfortunately, a blast of noise from the Experience Resort fee $20/day. Mon–Thurs & Sun $24, Fri & Sat $99.

GOLDEN NUGGET > 129 E Fremont St ☎ 800 634 3454 or ☎ 702 385 7111, Ⓦ goldennugget.com. MAP P.87, POCKET MAP G12. Downtown's classiest option is the only hotel hereabouts with amenities – like its amazing pool – to match the Strip giants. The actual rooms, at their freshest but loudest in the Rush Tower overlooking Fremont Street, are smart and comfortable, if not all that exciting. Resort fee $27.50/day. Mon–Thurs & Sun $49, Fri & Sat $124.

LAS VEGAS HOSTEL > 1322 E Fremont St ☏ 800 550 8958 or ☏ 702 385 1150, Ⓦ lasvegashostel.net. MAP P.87, POCKET MAP J13. Popular with young travellers, this converted motel is almost a mile east of downtown in an area where walking is unadvisable. Adequate bare-bones accommodation includes four-, six- and eight-bed single-sex and mixed dorms, and en-suite private rooms. There's also a pool, hot tub and organized activities. Wi-fi, parking and breakfast included. Dorms $15–25/person; doubles $40.

MAIN STREET STATION > 200 N Main St ☏ 800 465 0711 or ☏ 702 387 1896, Ⓦ www.mainstreetcasino.com. MAP P.87, POCKET MAP G11. A short but safe walk north of Fremont Street, this large and reasonably modern casino is always good value, for accommodation, food and drink; it's particularly good as an affordable base for a busy weekend. Ask for a room away from the interstate. No resort fee. Mon–Thurs & Sun $40, Fri & Sat $100.

THE PLAZA > 1 Main St ☏ 800 634 6575 or ☏ 702 386 2110, Ⓦ www .plazahotelcasino.com. MAP P.87, POCKET MAP F11. The veteran Plaza, at the end of Fremont Street on the site of Las Vegas's original railroad station, pulled off a real coup in 2011. It bought up the brand-new fixtures and fittings from the prestigious Fontainebleu on the Strip, so badly hit by the recession it never even opened, and used them to turn its run-down rooms into some of the smartest and best-value lodgings around. Resort fee $18/day. Mon–Thurs & Sun $35, Fri & Sat $99.

The rest of the city

GOLD COAST > 4000 W Flamingo Rd, ☏ 888 402 6278 or ☏ 702 367 7111, Ⓦ www.goldcoastcasino.com. MAP P.95, POCKET MAP G15. Sedate, old-fashioned locals casino, complete with bingo and a bowling alley, a hot half-mile west of the Strip (to which it's connected by free shuttle buses), but right by the fancier Rio and Palms. The rooms are not at all bad, but there's no earthly reason to stay unless the price is right. Resort fee $18/day. Mon–Thurs & Sun $45, Fri & Sat $115.

HARD ROCK HOTEL > 4455 Paradise Rd ☏ 800 473 7625, Ⓦ www.hardrockhotel .com. MAP P.95, POCKET MAP B16. If you know what you're coming for – to mix with partying 20-somethings – the Hard Rock will suit you perfectly. The rooms are cool and comfortable, and you can even open the floor-to-ceiling windows. It's too far from the Strip, though, to make a good base for seeing the city as a whole. Weekends book up early; reserve in advance. Resort fee $28/day. Mon–Thurs & Sun $70, Fri & Sat $279.

ORLEANS > 4500 W Tropicana Ave ☏ 800 675 3267 or ☏ 702 365 7111, Ⓦ www.orleanscasino.com. MAP P.95, POCKET MAP A12. Provided you get one of its freshly renovated rooms and you have a car to get around, the Orleans, a mile west of the Strip, can serve as an affordable base to explore Las Vegas. The on-site cinema is a real boon. Resort fee $18/day. Mon–Thurs & Sun $50, Fri & Sat $128.

THE PALMS > 4321 W Flamingo Rd ☏ 866 942 7777 or ☏ 702 942 7777, Ⓦ palms.com. MAP P.95, POCKET MAP F16. One of the very few off-Strip casinos that you might genuinely want to stay in, rather than simply find a good-value rate for, the Palms is renowned for its clubs, gigs and weekend buzz. Things are much quieter on weekdays, but with such comfortable rooms and great pools, it can be a real bargain. Resort fee $30/day. Mon–Thurs & Sun $89, Fri & Sat $169.

RIO > 3700 W Flamingo Rd ☏ 866 746 7671, Ⓦ www.caesars.com/rio-las -vegas. MAP P.95, POCKET MAP H15. Part of the Caesars Entertainment empire, but separated by half a mile from its Strip siblings, the Rio really isn't a bad accommodation option. As well as high-class amenities and entertainment, it offers comfortable rooms (large but not suites, as they claim). The Palms is over the road, but you may feel you're missing out on all the action. Resort fee $29/day. Mon–Thurs & Sun $69, Fri & Sat $149.

SAM'S TOWN > 5111 Boulder Hwy ☏ 800 897 8696 or ☏ 702 456 7777, Ⓦ www.samstownlv.com. MAP P.95, POCKET MAP D12. Quietly prospering from meeting its middle-American customers' needs with Wild West shops, restaurants and bars, this old-fashioned locals casino stands resolutely apart from modern Las Vegas. If you want to dip into town but stay somewhere more peaceful, its comfortable rooms may suit you fine. It's a six-mile shuttle ride to the Strip so you're better off with a car. **Resort fee $16/day. Mon–Thurs & Sun $42, Fri & Sat $105.**

SUNSET STATION > 1301 W Sunset Rd, Henderson ☎ 888 786 7389 or ☎ 702 547 7777, ⓦ sunsetstation .com. MAP P.95, POCKET MAP D13. This huge, attractive and well-equipped casino, ten miles southeast of the Strip en route towards Arizona, would seem impressive anywhere else. Here, despite its pool and fine restaurants, it counts as low-key, and only worth considering if the price is right or you're passing by. **Resort fee $19/day. Mon–Thurs & Sun $55, Fri & Sat $150.**

WESTGATE LAS VEGAS RESORT > 3000 Paradise Rd ☎ 702 732 5111, ⓦ westgateresorts.com. MAP P.95, POCKET MAP L5. How the mighty are fallen. The only reason to stay in the former Hilton – once, as home to Elvis, Las Vegas's premier hotel – is if you're attending a convention next door. Otherwise, the rooms just aren't good enough to compensate for the cut-off location and general air of decay. **Resort fee $30/day. Mon–Thurs & Sun $65, Fri & Sat $136.**

Mount Charleston

MOUNT CHARLESTON LODGE > 5375 Kyle Canyon Rd ☎ 702 872 5408, ⓦ mtcharlestonlodge.com. MAP PP.104–105. Nineteen comfortably appointed log cabins, alongside the restaurant (see p.111) at the far end of Hwy-157. Lacking phones, wi-fi and TV reception, they're especially popular with honeymooners escaping Las Vegas. **$130.**

RESORT ON MOUNT CHARLESTON > 2 Kyle Canyon Rd ☎ 888 559 1888, ☎ 702 872 5500, ⓦ mtcharlestonresort.com. MAP PP.104–105. Set below Hwy-157, facing a towering rocky outcrop 17 miles up from US-95, the best accommodation option in the mountains holds 61 cosy, smart rooms, arranged around an artificial lake. **$85.**

Grand Canyon South Rim

BRIGHT ANGEL LODGE > Grand Canyon South Rim, AZ. Advance reservations ☎ 888 297 2757 or ☎ 303 297 2757, same-day reservations ☎ 928 638 2631, ⓦ grandcanyonlodges.com. MAP PP.104–105. Stretching along the South Rim and consisting of a grand lodge flanked by individual cabins, this fantastic-value option is usually booked up months in advance. Some units share bathrooms, while others enjoy canyon views. **Double with shared bathroom $93.**

EL TOVAR > Grand Canyon South Rim, AZ. Advance reservations ☎ 888 297 2757 or ☎ 303 297 2757, same-day reservations ☎ 928 638 2631, ⓦ www.grandcanyonlodges.com. MAP PP.104–105. At heart an overgrown log cabin, this magnificent, century-old hotel, a symphony in dark wood, is the definitive national park lodge. Although it's very close to the rim, only three of its 78 rooms offer substantial canyon views. **$207.**

Zion National Park

DESERT PEARL INN > 707 Zion Park Blvd, Springdale UT ☎ 888 828 0898 or ☎ 435 772 8888, ⓦ desertpearl .com. MAP PP.104–105. An absolutely gorgeous hotel, ranged alongside the Virgin River just outside the park, with superb views. From the parking areas it may look like a regular motel, but the actual rooms are huge, modern and very attractive, and there's a good pool with hot tubs. **$249.**

ZION LODGE > Zion National Park, UT. Advance reservations ☎ 888 297 2757 or ☎ 303 297 2757, same-day reservations ☎ 435 772 7700, ⓦ www .zionlodge.com. MAP PP.104–105. The only accommodation option inside the national park, occupying pride of place on lush lawns in the heart of the Canyon. The forty en-suite cabins have gas fireplaces and private porches, while the 72 motel rooms are plainer, but still have porches or balconies. **Cabins $210, motel rooms $220.**

Arrival

A very high proportion of visitors to Las Vegas **fly** into the city's only significant airport, not far east of the Strip, while all the rest **drive** across the empty desert from elsewhere in the USA. No passenger trains currently serve the city, though there's talk of constructing a high-speed link with Los Angeles.

By air

Las Vegas's ever-expanding **McCarran International Airport** (☏702 261 5211, ⊚www.mccarran .com) lies immediately southeast of the Strip; aircraft pass within a mile of Mandalay Bay and the Tropicana as they taxi. However, both its terminals – confusingly numbered 1 and 3, since the new Terminal 3, used by all international flights, replaced the former Terminal 2 in 2012 – are accessed from the east, via Paradise Road. That means the closest Strip casinos are around three miles by road from the airport; the Venetian and Wynn more like five miles; and downtown hotels around seven miles.

Assuming you're not renting a car – in which case, note that all the rental companies are based at a separate, off-site facility (see p.126) – much the best way to transfer from the airport to your hotel is by **taxi**. In principle, a cab ride to the southern Strip (10–20min) will cost $16 and upwards, and to the northern Strip (20–30min) more like $30. If the traffic's bad you may have to pay up to $10 more.

Lone travellers may prefer to pay for a seat in a shared **Bell Trans shuttle bus** (☏702 386 7494, ⊚bell-trans.com), which costs $7.50 to the Strip and $10 to downtown, but as these services drop off other passengers en route the journey time can be long, an hour or more for properties on the North Strip.

It is also possible, but even slower, to use the **RTC bus network** (see p.125), by taking route #109 from the airport to the South Strip Transfer Terminal, and changing there onto the Strip And Downtown Express, for a total fare of $3. The total journey is likely to take at least half an hour for the South Strip, and over an hour for the North Strip and downtown.

Note that the **Las Vegas Monorail** (see p.126) does not serve the airport.

By car

The main driving route into Las Vegas is the **I-15** interstate, which connects the city with Los Angeles, 270 miles southwest, and Salt Lake City, 420 miles northeast. On Fridays especially, it tends to be clogged with cars arriving from southern California. Only if traffic is at a standstill is it worth leaving the interstate before you reach the exit closest to your final destination. If you're coming from California, therefore, you wouldn't normally expect to drive the full length of Las Vegas Boulevard, which runs parallel to I-15 from the southern end of the valley, and becomes the Strip roughly ten miles along.

Driving to Las Vegas from the Grand Canyon or anywhere else in Arizona, you'll approach the city along **US-93**, via the Hoover Dam. Either follow the same road, as Boulder Highway, all the way to downtown, or turn west, most likely on Tropicana Road or Flamingo Avenue, to reach the Strip.

By bus

Long-distance **Greyhound buses** (☏800 231 2222, ⊚www.greyhound .com), which connect Las Vegas with other Southwestern cities including Los Angeles, Phoenix and Salt Lake City, stop downtown rather than on the Strip. The station is alongside the Plaza hotel, at 200 S Main Street.

Getting around

If you're visiting Las Vegas specifically to spend time on the Strip and/or downtown – as most visitors do – there's no point renting a car. Downtown is small enough to walk around, while a good **bus service** runs the length of the Strip and continues to downtown, and there are also several separate **monorail systems** on the Strip. Only if you expect to explore further afield – to outlying areas (see p.94), or to the surrounding desert (see p.104) – does a car become essential.

On foot

It comes as a big surprise to most visitors quite how much **walking** you have to do in Las Vegas. The Strip might look like a simple straight line on the map, but it has a peculiar geography all of its own; the colossal scale of the buildings tricks the eye, making them look smaller and nearer than they really are. Each individual casino can measure a mile end to end, while walking from, say, a restaurant in one property to a club in the next can take half an hour. Especially in summer, when the searing heat makes it all but impossible to walk more than a block or two outdoors plotting a route from A to B becomes a real art, involving cutting through air-conditioned casinos, catching the occasional monorail and other such dodges.

By bus

While **RTC buses** (wcatride.com) cover the whole city, two routes meet almost all visitors' needs. Buy tickets before boarding; machines at stops along both routes sell passes for 2 hours ($6), 24 hours ($8) or 3 days ($20). All buses have wheelchair access

The **Deuce on the Strip** (daily 24hr) runs the full length of the Strip, from Mandalay Bay to the Stratosphere, stopping outside all the casinos, and also loops around downtown, running north on Casino Center Boulevard and south on Las Vegas Boulevard. While its principal downtown stop is where the Fremont Street Experience meets Las Vegas Boulevard, it also stops in both directions at the Bonneville Transit Center (BTC), six blocks south at Bonneville and Casino Center, the main interchange for crosstown routes.

As the name suggests, the faster **Strip & Downtown Express**, or SDX, (daily 9am–midnight) also connects the Strip with downtown, but with fewer stops. In addition, rather than follow the Strip between Wynn Las Vegas and the Stratosphere, it detours west to run past the Convention Center. Downtown, the most useful stop is where the Fremont Street Experience meets Casino Center Boulevard, though the route loops back west beyond Fremont Street to terminate at the Las Vegas Premium Outlets (North) mall, and it also stops at the Bonneville Transit Center. Southbound SDX buses stop on the Strip outside the Fashion Show Mall, Bellagio, Excalibur and Mandalay Bay; northbound buses stop across from Mandalay Bay, and outside the MGM Grand, Paris and Wynn. The southern end of the route is the South Strip Transfer Terminal (SSTT), three miles southeast of Mandalay Bay at 6675 Gilespie Street, which connects with other bus routes and is also served by free airport shuttle buses.

In addition, various free **shuttle buses** connect the Strip with further-flung casinos. From Harrah's, buses run west to the Rio (every 30min, daily 10am–1am; ☎800 214 9110) and east to Sam's Town (every 1hr 30min, daily 9.30am–9.30pm; ☎800 897 8696). From the intersection of Flamingo Road with the Strip, buses run via the Gold Coast to the Orleans (half-hourly departures, daily 9.30am–12.30am).

By monorail

Four separate monorail systems currently operate along different stretches of the Strip. The longest, but in some respects least useful, is the one officially called the **Las Vegas Monorail** (Mon 7am–midnight, Tues–Thurs 7am–2am, Fri–Sun 7am–3am; single trip $5, 1-day pass $12, 3-day pass $28; ⊙www.lvmonorail.com). It runs behind the casinos on the eastern side of the Strip, from the MGM Grand to SLS Las Vegas, detouring east en route to call at the Convention Center. Had the route been extended south to the airport, and downtown in the north, it could have relieved Las Vegas's traffic problems. As it is, it's only conceivably helpful for hops along the southern Strip. Even then, all the stations are located right at the back of the relevant casinos, ten minutes' walk from their Strip entrances, so it can be slower to catch the Monorail than to walk.

All the other three monorail systems are **free**, and link small groups of neighbouring casinos. The southernmost connects Mandalay Bay with Excalibur, via Luxor. The second runs from the Monte Carlo, via Aria and Crystals in CityCenter, to Bellagio; it's a futuristic ride, but be warned that the Bellagio station is in that property's far southwestern corner, far from the casino floor and the Strip. Finally, there's the short link between the Mirage and TI now, which serves little practical function other than keeping pedestrians cool.

By car

Locals might find it hard to believe, but for visitors, **driving** in Las Vegas can be a real pleasure. The thrill of cruising along the Strip, with its sights and sounds and blazing signs, only wears thin if you're actually trying to get somewhere by a certain time. Tourists tend naturally to avoid the worst times for traffic, like the morning rush hour.

Recently, however, the major Strip casinos have broken with tradition by imposing sizeable **parking fees** on all visitors, even their own overnight guests ("resort fees" do not include parking). Typically set at $8 for a short visit, $13/day for self-parking, and more like $20/day for valet parking, it's a major disincentive to renting a car. Most downtown casinos charge non-guests for parking, often waived if you use their restaurants or bars.

Car rental is available from almost every Strip or downtown hotel; as a rule each holds one or two outlets of the major rental chains. However, you can find a much wider choice, and usually better rates, if you pick up at the airport. That said, the major rental agencies are no longer based at the airport itself, but at the **McCarran Rent-A-Car Center**, three miles southwest at 7135 Gilespie Street, which is connected with the terminals by free shuttle buses. If you're already in the city and decide to rent a car, be sure to take a cab direct to the Rent-A-Car Center. Expect to pay around $40 per day, or $200 per week, for a compact car.

By taxi

Since Strip casinos started to charge parking fees, services such as Uber and Lyft have boomed in Las Vegas, and are readily available throughout the city. As for traditional **taxis**, you can't hail one on the street, but long lines of cabs wait at the airport, and at casino entrances. Meters calculate fares at $3.50 for the first mile and $2.76 for each additional mile, but also run if you're delayed in traffic, charging $1.08 every two minutes. There's an additional $2 surcharge for trips to or from the airport (see p.124). Fifteen percent is the usual tip for the driver.

Gambling

Gambling, or as they like to call it these days "**gaming**", lies at the root of everything in Las Vegas. Only one visitor in ten doesn't gamble at all; the rest lose an average of $500 each in the casinos. Whether you're pumping coins into a slot machine or trying to beat the dealer at blackjack, the rules always mean the casino enjoys the "house edge". So long as you're 21 or over, and carrying ID to prove it, you can gamble anywhere you like. The glamour of the large **Strip casinos** can be seductive, but the minimum stake for each game tends to be higher, and the odds a little worse. Many visitors prefer to gamble **downtown**, where the atmosphere is a bit more down-and-dirty and their money holds out longer. Either way, decide in advance how much you're prepared to lose, and stop if you reach that point.

In all casinos waitresses will ply you with free drinks as long as you are gambling; tips are expected. If you gamble for any length of time, join the casino's free players club; it can earn you meals, freebies and future stays.

Baccarat

Formerly the preserve of high-rolling "whales", **baccarat** (pronounced bah-kah-rah) accounts for over forty percent of the casinos' revenue from table games. Played with an ordinary pack in which each numbered card counts its face value (aces are 1 not 11), except tens, jacks, queens and kings, all valued at zero, it's a simple game of luck. Only two hands are dealt, the "player" and the "bank". Each aims to reach a total value of nine; you can bet on either, but the bank has a slightly better chance of winning. The house advantage comes because the casino rakes off a small commission.

Blackjack

Also known as "21" or "pontoon", **blackjack** remains Las Vegas's favourite card game. Players compete against the bank, attempting to build a hand that adds nearly, or exactly, to 21. Tens, jacks, queens and kings count as ten points, aces as either one or eleven. Players make their bets before receiving two cards, then each in turn plays their hand through to completion, saying "hit" to receive additional cards, and either "stand" to stop, or "bust" if the total exceeds 21. The dealer plays last, according to fixed rules that preclude individual judgement. The house advantage comes because players who go bust lose their stakes whether or not the dealer does too. Players can minimize that advantage by learning the "correct" response to every situation – it's so hard that some casinos happily provide gamblers with the relevant charts.

Craps

If you don't know how to play the dice game **craps**, played on a high-walled baize table, take a lesson (freely available in most casinos) – you'll never be able to learn it from watching. The basic idea is that a different "shooter" throws a pair of dice each time around. Players bet on either "pass" or "don't pass" before the first throw, known as the "come-out roll". If that throw is 7 or 11, "pass" has won; if it's 2, 3 or 12, "don't pass" wins. Anything else, and the shooter throws again, and keeps doing so until either matching the original throw – a win for "pass" – or throwing 7 – a win for "don't pass". All sorts of side bets capture the imaginations of serious gamblers.

Poker

In **poker**, players compete against each other, not the house, to build the best five-card hand (see box, p.128). The two most popular variations are

Seven Card Stud, in which each player receives two cards face down, four face up, and then the last face down, and Texas Hold 'Em, in which your two face-down cards are supplemented by five face-up communal cards. The casino rakes off a percentage of each pot. You're therefore playing against whoever else happens to be around; it's possible to win, but it's a big risk to assume you're the best player at the table.

Casinos also offer what's effectively poker played in a **blackjack format**, in which each player attempts to beat the dealer. Formats include Let It Ride, Pai Gow Poker and Caribbean Stud.

Roulette

Roulette is the game in which a ball lands in a numbered slot in a rotating wheel. You can bet on the specific number, or group of numbers, and if the slot is "red" or "black". Winners are paid as though the wheel holds 36 slots, but it usually holds 38, thanks to two green slots, 0 and 00. Always look for wheels that hold only one zero slot, and thus offer better odds. You can't get your money back by repeatedly redoubling your stake; tables only allow bets up to a quickly reached maximum.

Slot machines

Casinos make more money from **slot machines** than from anything else. All machines are programmed to pay out a percentage of their intake as winnings. On average, visitors feed $1600 per day into every single machine in the city, and win $1500 back again, leaving the casino $100 profit. The slots downtown offer better odds than on the Strip.

A "non-progressive" machine always pays the same for a specific winning combination and pays smaller but more frequent jackpots. "Progressive" slots, such as Wheel of Fortune, are linked into networks where the overall jackpot can climb into millions of dollars, before someone scoops the lot.

Video poker is an addictive cross between traditional slot machines and the table game. The odds can be so good that on certain machines, players who play a perfect strategy have a slight advantage over the house.

Sports betting

Las Vegas is all but unique in the USA in offering visitors the chance to bet on sports events legally, in the highly charged atmosphere of a major casino. Almost every casino holds either a **Sports Book**, or if it covers horseracing as well, a **Race and Sports Book**, which vary from comfortable high-tech lounges to something more like a raucous neighbourhood sports bar. All offer much the same odds on any specific event and many offer "in-running" wagering, meaning moment-by-moment bets on games currently in progress.

Ranking of poker hands

Straight flush Five consecutive cards in the same suit.
Four of a kind Four aces, four sevens, etc.
Full house Three of a kind and a separate pair.
Flush Any five cards in the same suit.
Straight Five consecutive cards not in the same suit.
Three of a kind Three kings, three sixes, etc.
Two pair Two fours and two jacks, etc.
One pair Two tens, etc.

Directory A–Z

Cinemas

Typical ticket prices for cinemas in Las Vegas are around $8 for matinee performances, starting before 6pm, and $10 for evening shows.

AMC Town Square 18 Town Square, 6587 Las Vegas Blvd S ☎702 362 7283, ⓦwww.amctheatres.com.

Brenden Theatres & IMAX The Palms, 4321 W Flamingo Rd ☎702 507 4849, ⓦwww.brendentheatres.com.

Century 18 Orleans, 4500 W Tropicana Ave ☎702 889 1220, ⓦwww.cinemark.com.

Century 18 Sam's Town, 5111 Boulder Hwy ☎702 547 1732, ⓦwww.cinemark.com.

Regal 13 Sunset Station, 1301 W Sunset Rd, Henderson ☎702 221 2283, ⓦwww.regmovies.com.

United Artists Showcase 8 Next door to the MGM Grand at 3769 Las Vegas Blvd S ☎702 221 2283, ⓦwww.regmovies.com. The only cinema on the Strip.

Crime

While you're safe in the major public spaces of Las Vegas, such as inside the security-conscious casinos, crime can be a problem elsewhere. Away from the crowded Strip, which has its own problems with **pickpockets** and bag-snatchers, you can feel exposed and vulnerable if you walk any distance outdoors. It's essential to keep your cash hidden at all times, not to flaunt valuables like cameras and iPads, and not to tell strangers your hotel room number. Be cautious in multistorey parking garages, especially at night, and try to park close to the exits.

Electricity

The **electricity** supply in Las Vegas, as in all of the USA, is 110 volts AC, and uses two-pin plugs. Bring or buy an adapter, and if necessary a voltage converter as well, if you're travelling from a country that uses a different system and need to use your own electrical appliances.

Health

In any medical emergency call ☎911. The front desk or phone operator at your hotel will be able to advise on sources of appropriate help.

Hospitals that have 24hr emergency rooms include Sunrise Hospital, 3186 S Maryland Parkway (☎702 731 8000, ⓦsunrise-hospital.com), and the University Medical Center, 1800 W Charleston Blvd (☎702 383 2000, ⓦwww.umcsn.com). For more minor issues, head to the Harmon Medical Center, 150 E Harmon Ave (Mon–Fri 8am–8pm; ☎702 796 1116).

Twenty-four-hour **pharmacies** on the Strip include the 24hr CVS Pharmacy, alongside the Monte Carlo at 3758 Las Vegas Blvd S (☎702 262 9284) and Walgreens, beside the main Palazzo entrance at 3339 Las Vegas Blvd S (☎702 369 8166).

To find a local **dentist**, contact the Nevada Dental Association (☎702 255 4211, ⓦnvda.org).

Internet

Every casino/hotel in Las Vegas provides in-room **wi-fi** access for its guests, but only rarely is it free. In almost all cases, internet access forms the largest component of the compulsory "resort fee" (see box, p.115), which typically costs at least $20 per day, and may well cover one device only; elsewhere, hotel guests can generally choose to pay a stand-alone fee of around $15 per day. On top of that, if you're spending time in a casino other than one you're staying in, you won't normally have wi-fi access.

Several casinos, however, including most of the MGM Resorts properties, offer **free wi-fi** access to everyone in their public areas, as opposed to the guest rooms. In addition, a handful of shops and cafés along the Strip provide free wi-fi to customers (and anyone who happens to be in the immediate vicinity): *Coffee Bean & Tea Leaf* in Planet Hollywood's Miracle Mile (see p.62); and the Apple Store and *Starbucks* in the Fashion Show Mall (see p.77).

Free wi-fi is also available throughout McCarran International Airport.

LGBT travellers

Although Las Vegas, or at least the parts of the city that visitors are at all likely to see, is a **gay-friendly** city, the casinos make little show of catering to gay travellers in any specific sense. No Strip casino currently holds a specifically gay club, so the city's gay-oriented nightlife focuses instead around what's fondly known as the "**Fruit Loop**", a mile east of the Strip, where Paradise Road, running south from the Hard Rock, meets Naples Drive. Well-known clubs in the neighbourhood include Piranha (see p.103), but there are none exclusively geared towards women.

The best source of information on current issues and events in Las Vegas's gay community is the monthly magazine *QVegas*, distributed in a free printed version and also available online (gayvegas.com).

Since same-sex marriage was declared legal in Nevada in 2014, the major casino chapels have rushed to offer gay wedding ceremonies, even if certain private chapels have refused. The **Gay Chapel of Las Vegas**, 1205 Las Vegas Blvd S (702 384 0771, gaychapelof lasvegas.com) offers a full range of ceremonies; Elvis is optional.

The annual **Las Vegas Pride** event, celebrated in late October (866 930 3336, lasvegaspride .org), kicks off with a Friday night parade through downtown, while the Saturday sees an open-air festival in Sunset Park, at the corner of Sunset Road and Eastern Avenue, 10 miles south of downtown.

In May, the **Nevada Gay Rodeo Association** (ngra.com) holds the three-day BigHorn Rodeo at Horseman's Park, 5800 E Flamingo Rd.

Money

Las Vegas is not a budget destination in any meaningful sense. The days are gone when casinos used cut-price food and entertainment to lure in gamblers. Now everything from restaurants to showrooms have to make a profit, and prices are high. A typical all-you-can-eat buffet costs $20 or more for dinner; a run-of-the-mill restaurant more like $40 per head, without drinks; and a gourmet place double that or more. Tickets for a show can easily cost $100 or more, while a night out in a big club is liable to cost hundreds, and potentially thousands, of dollars. Hotel room rates are generally good value, and on weekdays compare favourably with what you'd get for the same money elsewhere in the USA, but can run into hundreds per night on weekends. On top of that, of course, the average visitor also loses several hundred dollars gambling.

As for how you bring your money, it's assumed everywhere that you'll use a **credit card** for all significant expenses. It's extremely easy to get cash anywhere on the Strip; ATMs are everywhere, though all tend to charge around $3 for withdrawals.

Travellers from overseas are advised not to bring foreign cash; there are no banks on the Strip, and while the casinos will gladly change your cash you won't get a good rate. Dollar **travellers' cheques** are accepted as cash everywhere, though few visitors bring them these days.

Phones

Foreign visitors can assume that their **mobile phones** (cell phones) will work in Las Vegas, though it's worth checking with your phone provider that your existing payment scheme will cover you there, and what the call charges are. Many providers offer short-term pricing packages designed to make holiday phone usage more affordable. If you plan to access the internet using your phone, make sure that you know your provider's roaming charges, which may well be extremely expensive.

For all calls, you can make tremendous savings by using **Skype**, or similar programmes, to make free wi-fi calls from your phone or laptop. Alternatively, prepaid **phone cards** are widely available from casino convenience stores, petrol (gas) stations, supermarkets and other outlets. Many casinos, especially those that charge resort fees (see p.115), offer guests free local phone calls; making an international call from your hotel room phone is always liable to be very expensive.

Smoking

Smoking remains legal in the public areas of all casinos, and in bars that do not serve food. It is forbidden in restaurants, including those inside casinos, though smoke does waft into those restaurants that are open to the casino floor. All hotels offer non-smoking rooms.

Emergency numbers

In any medical or security emergency, call ☎911.

Tax

Sales tax of 8.15 percent is charged on all purchases in Las Vegas. Hotel rates are subject to an additional **room tax** of twelve percent on the Strip, and thirteen percent downtown (see box, p.115).

Time

Las Vegas is in the **Pacific Time Zone**, three hours behind the Eastern Time Zone. It's almost always seven hours behind the UK, though clocks in the US move forward by one hour on the second Sunday in March and back one hour on the first Sunday in November, placing them briefly out of synch with clocks in the UK.

Tipping

Tipping etiquette is not as complicated as many visitors imagine; if you find yourself wondering whether to tip, do. Servers in restaurants depend on tips for their income, and expect at least fifteen percent. So do cab drivers. If someone carries your bags, tip $1–2 per bag; valet parking attendants expect $2; and it's usual to leave a tip of $1 or $2 per day when you leave your hotel room. When gambling, it's considered appropriate to tip the dealer a chip or two if you win. Bar staff, or casino waitresses bringing free drinks, expect $1–2 per drink.

Tourist information

The best single source of information on the city is ⊕lasvegas.com, the website of the **Las Vegas Convention and Visitor Authority** (LVCVA). They also run a visitor centre at 3150 Paradise Rd, half a mile east of the Strip (Mon–Fri 8am–5pm; ☎877 847 4858), but it holds nothing you can't find much more easily elsewhere.

Other useful websites include: ⊕dmckee.lvablog.com The "Stiffs and Georges" blog is a lively but

131

serious source of news and comment on Las Vegas and the casino industry.

Ⓦ **www.eatinglv.com** This long-running blog holds a huge archive of restaurant reviews.

Ⓦ **www.everythinglv.com** Weekly online updates on the latest Las Vegas news, plus reader forums.

Ⓦ **lasvegassun.com** Las Vegas's best daily newspaper website.

Ⓦ **lasvegasweekly.com** A good source of current listings, plus a handy archive of their annual "Best of Las Vegas" awards in all sorts of categories.

Ⓦ **www.lvol.com** Schedules, reservations and reviews for concerts and shows; a good place to find out what's happening while you're in town.

Travellers with disabilities

The **Las Vegas Convention and Visitors Authority** offers detailed advice for disabled visitors; download the Access Las Vegas brochure from Ⓦ lasvegas.com, or call their advice line on ☎702 892 0711.

All the casinos in Las Vegas are **wheelchair accessible** and offer hotel rooms designed to suit visitors with disabilities. Don't underestimate the sheer scale of each casino, let alone the Strip as a whole; an individual destination like a restaurant or a theatre may be a long way from the nearest parking space. If you need to rent specific mobility equipment, contact Ability Center, 6001 S Decatur Blvd (☎702 434 3030, Ⓦwww.abilitycenter.com). For public transport, both Bell Trans shuttle buses from the airport (☎702 739 7990, Ⓦbell-trans.com) and RTC buses in the city itself (Ⓦcatride.com) are wheelchair accessible. If you plan to drive yourself, note that the national rental chains offer adapted vehicles, and visitors can arrange temporary free **disabled**

parking permits via the Nevada Department of Motor Vehicles (☎775 684 4750, Ⓦwww.dmvnv.com).

Tours

Las Vegas does not offer the kind of **sightseeing tours** familiar in other cities. Almost everything of interest in the city itself is in and around the casinos; you can't really appreciate them from a passing bus, and they're too big to explore more than one or two at a time on foot. **Bus tours** do, however, head further afield. Thus Gray Line (☎702 739 7777, Ⓦwww.grayline.com) offers tours to the Hoover Dam (4hr 30min; $65); the Grand Canyon West Rim (11hr; $149); and the Grand Canyon South Rim (14hr; $175). Helicopter operators, including Maverick (☎702 261 0007, Ⓦwww.maverickhelicopter.com) and Sundance (☎702 736 0606, Ⓦwww.sundancehelicopters.com), offer brief day or night **"flight-seeing" tours** over the Strip, at typical prices of around $100 for a flight lasting less than fifteen minutes. They and other companies also fly day-trippers east to the Grand Canyon (see box, p.108).

Travelling with children

In the early 1990s, Las Vegas flirted briefly with the idea that it might become a child-friendly destination to match Orlando, Florida. That dream was swiftly abandoned; gambling and kids don't make a good mix. Even so, many visitors bring their **kids** to the city; the Strip sidewalk is thronged until after midnight with parents pushing cumbersome buggies and struggling with exhausted children.

There's still a lot about Las Vegas that will appeal to kids, from the castles and pyramids, volcanoes and fountains on the Strip, to more specific paying attractions. Among the most popular with children are the Secret Garden and Dolphin Habitat at the Mirage; Shark Reef at Mandalay Bay; the Bodies and Titanic exhibitions at Luxor; the gondolas at the Venetian; CSI: The Experience at the MGM Grand; and the roller coasters and thrill rides at New York–New York, Circus Circus and the Stratosphere.

All the casinos welcome children as guests. Strictly speaking, **under-21s** are not allowed in gambling areas, which means that family groups have to keep walking rather than linger on the casino floor. Casinos do not offer babysitting services, but can provide details of babysitting agencies.

Note that in many casinos, some or all of the swimming pools now operate as adults-only "dayclubs", with drinking, dancing and partying; it's worth checking in advance before you go ahead and book your accommodation.

Weddings

Thanks to Nevada's notoriously minimal legal requirements, and especially the lack of an obligatory waiting period, around a quarter of a million people get married in Las Vegas each year.

At its simplest, arranging a Vegas wedding is very straightforward. First of all, you need a **Nevada marriage licence**. To get that, both parties must appear in person at the Clark County Marriage Bureau, 201 E Clark Ave, downtown (daily 8am–midnight; ☎702 671 0600, ⊚www.clarkcountynv.gov). So long as both are aged 18 or over, not married already and can show picture ID, they'll sell you a licence for $77 (credit cards $82, debit cards not accepted). Note that there isn't an office on the Strip.

If you've made an advance reservation, you can then walk with your licence to the office of the **Commissioner of Civil Marriages**, on the sixth floor at 330 S Third St (Mon–Thurs 2–6pm, Fri 9.30am–8.45pm, Sat 12.30–8.45pm, Sun 9am–5pm; ☎702 671 0577, ⊚www.clarkcountynv.gov) and pay another $75 cash to have the actual ceremony performed. One witness is required; ideally you should bring your own, though what the Commissioner charmingly calls "unsavoury individuals" lurk outside the offices, hoping to sell their services as witnesses.

Just because it's possible to have a quick, cheap wedding in Las Vegas, however, doesn't mean that's what most couples actually do. Instead, most marriages are celebrated in wedding chapels, which can be stand-alone structures of the kind reviewed throughout this book or yet another component in the huge casino-hotels. You can find full listings of chapels and wedding planners on the official Las Vegas CVB website, ⊚www .lasvegas.com, and also on the casinos' own websites.

Prices at **wedding chapels** range upwards from around $200 all-in for a bare-bones ceremony. For the full works, which in Las Vegas can include helicopter flights to the Grand Canyon or pretty much anything else you care to mention, the bill can of course run into thousands of dollars. The biggest hidden expense is likely to be photography; be sure to check whether you or your guests will be allowed to bring cameras, and if not, how much the official photos or footage will cost.

Finally, note that now **gay marriage** has become legal in Nevada all the major casino chapels, and most but not all of the private chapels, are happy to perform gay weddings. For more details, see p.130

Festivals

Compared to other American cities, Las Vegas does not have an extensive calendar of annual events. In terms of attracting crowds, the biggest events tend to be the opening of new casinos and, even more exciting, the implosions of old ones.

NASCAR WEEKEND

Early March ⓦwww.lvms.com
Three days of racing at the Las Vegas Motor Speedway, 7000 Las Vegas Blvd N at Speedway Blvd.

ST PATRICK'S DAY

March 17
Pubs, clubs, casinos and restaurants all celebrate St Patrick's Day.

WORLD SERIES OF POKER

Late May to mid-July ⓦpoker.wsop.com
The world's premier poker tournament has been held at the Rio since 1995.

LAS VEGAS HELLDORADO DAYS

Mid-May ⓦwww.elkshelldorado.com
Five nights of pro rodeo action in Symphony Park – at 100 S

Public holidays

Jan 1 New Year's Day
Jan 15 Martin Luther King Jr's Birthday
3rd Mon in Feb Presidents' Day
Last Mon in May Memorial Day
July 4 Independence Day
1st Mon in Sept Labor Day
2nd Mon in Oct Columbus Day
Nov 11 Veterans' Day
Last Thurs in Nov Thanksgiving Day
Dec 25 Christmas Day

Grand Central Parkway, alongside downtown's Smith Center – plus a Saturday night parade downtown.

NATIONAL FINALS RODEO

Early Dec ⓦnfrexperience.com
Ten-day pro rodeo event at the Thomas & Mack Center, 4505 S Maryland Parkway.

NEW YEAR'S EVE

December 31
The biggest night in the city's calendar, marked by concerts and festivities.

Conventions and trade shows

When planning a visit, it's useful to know when the city's biggest **conventions** are happening as room rates can soar.

Mid-Jan Consumer Electronics Show
Mid-Feb Men's Apparel Guild (MAGIC) convention
Early April National Association of Broadcasters convention
Mid-Aug Men's Apparel Guild (MAGIC) convention (again)
Early Nov Specialty Equipment Manufacturers Association (SEMA) convention

Chronology

1598 > Spain claims what's now southern Nevada as part of the colony of New Mexico.

1829 > Mexican explorers name an unexpected oasis of grasslands "Las Vegas" – "The Meadows".

1847 > USA acquires New Mexico.

1855 > Mormons establish the colony of Bringhurst in the Las Vegas Valley; it lasts three years.

1864 > Nevada becomes a state.

1905 > The railroad arrives. Las Vegas is established on May 15, when forty newly drawn blocks are auctioned.

1909 > Nevada becomes the first US state to outlaw gambling.

1931 > Nevada marks the end of Prohibition by legalizing gambling – the only state to do so.

1935 > Hoover Dam completed. Las Vegas hosts first convention.

1938 > Guy McAfee, former chief of LA's vice squad, takes over the Pair-O-Dice Club, on what he dubs "The Strip".

1940 > Las Vegas's population reaches eight thousand.

1941 > El Rancho opens as the Strip's first fully fledged resort.

1946 > Mobster "Bugsy" Siegel opens the Flamingo; he's murdered six months later after heavy losses.

1950s > An unstoppable flow of new Strip resorts includes the Desert Inn, the Sands, the Riviera, the Dunes and the Hacienda. Desert A-bomb tests can be seen and heard from the city.

1966 > Caesars Palace, the first themed casino, opens. Howard Hughes is asked to leave the Desert Inn because he isn't gambling; instead, he buys it, along with the Sands, the Silver Slipper and the New Frontier, marking the end of Mob domination.

1969 > Kirk Kerkorian opens the world's largest hotel– the Las Vegas Hilton – which hosts Elvis's rebirth as a karate-kicking lounge lizard.

1973 > Kirk Kerkorian again opens the world's largest hotel – the original MGM Grand, now Bally's. Steve Wynn takes over downtown's Golden Nugget.

1983 > Following disastrous fires at the MGM Grand and the Hilton, Las Vegas seems about to be eclipsed by Atlantic City; direct flights between New York and Las Vegas are discontinued.

1989 > Steve Wynn opens the opulent Mirage, complete with volcano. Benny Binion dies, with his Horseshoe downtown still Las Vegas's most profitable casino.

1993 > In a short-lived bid to reinvent Las Vegas as a child-friendly destination, Luxor, Treasure Island and the new MGM Grand all open.

1995 > Downtown roofed over to create Fremont Street Experience.

1997 > New York–New York opens; in a craze for building replica cities, it's followed by Bellagio in 1998 and the Venetian and Paris in 1999.

2005 > Harrah's buys Caesars Entertainment, leaving the Strip largely owned by two huge corporations. Wynn Las Vegas opens.

2009 > Despite recession, MGM Mirage completes CityCenter.

2011 > Carolyn Goodman succeeds her husband Oscar as mayor.

2014 > Las Vegas High Roller opens.

2015 > Caesars Entertainment goes into bankruptcy; emerges in 2016.

2016 > Venetian owner Sheldon Adelson is major donor to Donald Trump's presidential campaign.

PUBLISHING INFORMATION

This third edition published August 2017 by **Rough Guides Ltd**

80 Strand, London WC2R ORL

11, Community Centre, Panchsheel Park, New Delhi 110017, India

Distributed by Penguin Random House

Penguin Books Ltd, 80 Strand, London WC2R ORL

Penguin Group (USA) 345 Hudson Street, NY 10014, USA

Penguin Group (Australia) 250 Camberwell Road, Camberwell, Victoria 3124, Australia

Penguin Group (NZ) 67 Apollo Drive, Mairangi Bay, Auckland 1310, New Zealand

Penguin Group (South Africa) Block D, Rosebank Office Park, 181 Jan Smuts Avenue,

Parktown North, Gauteng, South Africa 2193

Rough Guides is represented in Canada by

DK Canada 320 Front Street West, Suite 1400, Toronto, Ontario M5V 3B6

Typeset in Minion and Din to an original design by Henry Iles and Dan May.

Printed and bound in China

© Rough Guides, 2017

Maps © Rough Guides

144pp includes index

A catalogue record for this book is available from the British Library

ISBN 978-0-24127-914-4

MIX
Paper from
responsible sources
FSC™ C018179
www.fsc.org

ROUGH GUIDES CREDITS

Editor: Olivia Rawes

Layout: Nikhil Agarwal

Cartography: Edward Wright

Picture editor: Marta Bescos

Photographer: Tim Draper

Proofreader: Susanne Hillen

Managing editor: Keith Drew

Production: Jimmy Lao

Cover photo research: Marta Bescos

Editorial assistant: Aimee White

Senior DTP coordinator: Dan May

Publishing director: Georgina Dee

THE AUTHOR

Greg Ward has been writing about Las Vegas for more than twenty years. As well as five previous Rough Guides to the city, he's the author of separate Rough Guides to the Southwest USA and the Grand Canyon. He has also written many other Rough Guides, including those to the USA, the *Titanic*, Hawaii, Brittany & Normandy, Provence, Spain, Blues CDs and US History; edited many more; and written books for several other publishers. For more information, visit ⓦ www.gregward.info.

ACKNOWLEDGEMENTS

Greg Ward: Thanks as ever to my dear wife Sam, for her support, encouragement and wise words. At Rough Guides, thanks to Olivia Rawes for her meticulous and eagle-eyed editing, and Ed Wright for his exceptional dedication to producing great maps. And thanks to everyone in Las Vegas who helped me to find and enjoy the very best of the city, especially Kimberley Diller and David Gonzalez, as well as Hannah Allen, Jennifer Byles, Stephanie Capelles, Stephanie Chavez, Katie Conway, Maggie Feldman, Sara Gorgon, Andrew Ho, Alison Monaghan Holly Olp, Jennifer Polito, Kellyann Roberts, Rochelle Samlin-Jurani, Josie Self, Melanie Shafer, Wendy Sloan, Eleni Stylianou, Melissa Warren and Cathy Wiedemer

HELP US UPDATE

We've gone to a lot of effort to ensure that the third edition of the **Pocket Rough Guide Las Vegas** is accurate and up-to-date. However, things change – places get "discovered", opening hours are notoriously fickle, restaurants and rooms raise prices or lower standards. If you feel we've got it wrong or left something out, we'd like to know, and if you can remember the address, the price, the hours, the phone number, so much the better.

Please send your comments with the subject line "**Pocket Rough Guide Las Vegas Update**" to mail@roughguides.com. We'll credit all contributions and send a copy of the next edition (or any other Rough Guide if you prefer) for the very best emails.

Find travel information, read inspiring features and book your trip on ⓦroughguides.com

Index

Maps are marked in **bold**.

R